6. Enter your class ID code to join a class.

### IF YOU HAVE A CLASS CODE FROM YOUR TEACHER

a. Enter your class code and click [ Next ]

b. Once you have joined a class, you will be able to use the Discussion Board and Email tools.

c. To enter this code later, choose **Join a Class**.

### IF YOU DO NOT HAVE A CLASS CODE

a. If you do not have a class ID code, click [ Skip ]

b. You do not need a class ID code to use *iQ Online*.

c. To enter this code later, choose **Join a Class**.

7. Review registration information and click Log In. Then choose your book. Click **Activities** to begin using *iQ Online*.

### IMPORTANT

• After you register, the next time you want to use *iQ Online*, go to www.iQOnlinePractice.com and log in with your email address and password.

• The online content can be used for 12 months from the date you register.

• For help, please contact customer service: eltsupport@oup.com.

## WHAT IS iQ ONLINE ?

All new activities provide essential skills **practice** and support.

Vocabulary and Grammar **games** immerse you in the language and provide even more practice.

Authentic, engaging **videos** generate new ideas and opinions on the Unit Question.

Go to the Media Center to download or stream all **student book audio**.

Use the **Discussion Board** to discuss the Unit Question and more.

**Email** encourages communication with your teacher and classmates.

**Automatic grading** gives immediate feedback and tracks progress.

**Progress Reports** show what you have mastered and where you still need more practice.

**OXFORD**
UNIVERSITY PRESS

198 Madison Avenue
New York, NY 10016 USA

Great Clarendon Street, Oxford, OX2 6DP, United Kingdom

Oxford University Press is a department of the University of Oxford.
It furthers the University's objective of excellence in research, scholarship,
and education by publishing worldwide. Oxford is a registered trade
mark of Oxford University Press in the UK and in certain other countries

Director, ELT New York: Laura Pearson
Head of Adult, ELT New York: Stephanie Karras
Publisher: Sharon Sargent
Managing Editor: Mariel DeKranis
Development Editor: Eric Zuarino
Executive Art and Design Manager: Maj-Britt Hagsted
Design Project Manager: Debbie Lofaso
Content Production Manager: Julie Armstrong
Senior Production Artist: Elissa Santos
Image Manager: Trisha Masterson
Image Editor: Liaht Ziskind
Production Coordinator: Brad Tucker

ISBN: 978 0 19 481870 4 Student Book 2 with iQ Online pack
ISBN: 978 0 19 481871 1 Student Book 2 as pack component
ISBN: 978 0 19 481802 5 iQ Online student website

Printed in China
This book is printed on paper from certified and well-managed sources.

ACKNOWLEDGEMENTS

*Although every effort has been made to trace and contact copyright holders before
publication, this has not been possible in some cases. We apologize for any apparent
infringement of copyright and if notified, the publisher will be pleased to rectify any
errors or omissions at the earliest opportunity.*

*The authors and publisher are grateful to those who have given permission to
reproduce the following extracts and adaptations of copyright material:*

p. 31 "The Color of Business" from "What Color Is Business?" by Orwig
Marketing Strategies. Copyright © 2004 Orwig Marketing Strategies,
http://www.orwig.net/articles/what_color/what_color.html. Used by
permission; p. 133 "I Hate Machines!" from "Self-Service World" by
Sheila Moss, http://www.humorcolumnist.com. Copyright Sheila Moss.
Used by permission; p. 158 from "In Praise of the Throwaway Society"
by Anthony Forte, http://www.madanthony.net. Used by permission of
the author.

*Illustrations by:* p. 76 Stuart Bradford; p. 86 5W Infographics; p. 126 Claudia
Carlson; p. 148 Karen Minot.

*We would also like to thank the following for permission to reproduce the following
photographs:* Cover: Yongyut Kumsri/Shutterstock; Inside back cover:
lvcandy/Getty Images, Bloom Design/shutterstock; Video Vocabulary (used
throughout the book): Oleksiy Mark / Shutterstock; p. 2 Ian Dagnall/
Alamy; p. 2/3 ericlefrancais/Shutterstock; p. 3 DrAfter123/iStockphoto
(media); p. 3 gbrundin/iStockphoto (listening); p. 6 Red Bull Content Pool/
Rex Features; p. 7 Courtesy of Tom Dickson and Blendtec/Blendtec;
p. 12 RichardBakerNews/Alamy; p. 13 Bloomberg/Getty Images; p. 26/27
Yongyut Kumsri/Shutterstock; p. 28 Tina Tyrell/Corbis Outline/Corbis UK
Ltd. (blue); p. 28 Tina Tyrell/Corbis Outline/Corbis UK Ltd. (brown); p. 28
Tina Tyrell/Corbis Outline/Corbis UK Ltd. (green); p. 28 Adam Blasberg/
Getty Images (red); p. 32 Henry Westheim Photography/Alamy; p. 37 Jim
West/Alamy; p. 41 Chris Rout/Alamy; p. 50/51 Brand New Images/Getty
Images; p. 54 Age Fotostock /Superstock Ltd.; p. 55 danishkhan /iStockphoto
(greeting); p. 55 Milk Photographie/Corbis UK Ltd. (gift); p. 61 David R.
Frazier Photolibrary, Inc./Alamy; p. 74/75 Stefan Holm/Shutterstock; p. 79
Natursports/Shutterstock; p. 85 Caiaimage/Rex Features; p. 98 mearicon/
Shutterstock (tools); p. 98 ColorBlind Images Blend Images/Newscom (father
son); p. 99 Jim Goldstein Danita Delimont Photography/Newscom (sign);
p. 99 Hurst Photo/Shutterstock (calculator); p. 100 amana images inc./Alamy
(family); p. 100 stockstudioX/Getty Images (kitchen); p. 100 Celia Peterson/
Getty Images (mother daughters); p. 100 Ken Seet/Corbis UK Ltd. (tucking
in); p. 103 Radius Images/Alamy; p. 104 2013 The Washington Post/Getty
Images; p. 109 Kristoffer Tripplaar/Alamy (sale); p. 109 Jerry Arcieri/Corbis
UK Ltd. (wall street); p. 122 Kevin Foy/Alamy; p. 123 master2/iStockphoto
(atm); p. 123 Alexandru Nika/Shutterstock (code); p. 124 Tim Boyle/Getty
Images (self-service); p. 124 Alex Segre/Alamy (tesco); p. 124 Henry George
Beeker/Alamy (airport); p. 124 Richard Levine/Alamy (gas); p. 134 Andres
Rodriguez/Alamy; p. 138 corepics/Fotolia; p. 139 Hugh Sitton/Corbis UK Ltd.;
p. 146/147 Jon Hicks/Corbis UK Ltd.; p. 151 Caro /Alamy (repair); p. 151 Peter
Crome/Alamy (mobile phones); p. 152 Photodisc/Oxford University Press;
p. 170 Matej Kastelic/Shutterstock; p. 170/171 piotr_pabijan/Shutterstock;
p. 171 OpenFlights (map); p. 171 Zoom Team/Shutterstock (fruit); p. 172
Halfdark/Getty Images (ill); p. 172 Nigel Cattlin /Alamy (mosquito); p. 172
Jose Luis Pelaez/Blend Images//Corbis UK Ltd. (xray); p. 172 Mark Hatfield/
Getty Images (test); p. 172 Brandon Tabiolo/Getty Images (sunscreen); p. 172
perfectmatch/Fotolia (inhaler).

# SHAPING learning TOGETHER

We would like to acknowledge the teachers from all over the world who participated in the development process and review of the Q series.

## Special thanks to our *Q: Skills for Success* Second Edition Topic Advisory Board

**Shaker Ali Al-Mohammad**, Buraimi University College, Oman; **Dr. Asmaa A. Ebrahim**, University of Sharjah, U.A.E.; **Rachel Batchilder**, College of the North Atlantic, Qatar; **Anil Bayir**, Izmir University, Turkey; **Flora Mcvay Bozkurt**, Maltepe University, Turkey; **Paul Bradley**, University of the Thai Chamber of Commerce Bangkok, Thailand; **Joan Birrell-Bertrand**, University of Manitoba, MB, Canada; **Karen E. Caldwell**, Zayed University, U.A.E.; **Nicole Hammond Carrasquel**, University of Central Florida, FL, U.S.; **Kevin Countryman**, Seneca College of Applied Arts & Technology, ON, Canada; **Julie Crocker**, Arcadia University, NS, Canada; **Marc L. Cummings**, Jefferson Community and Technical College, KY, U.S.; **Rachel DeSanto**, Hillsborough Community College Dale Mabry Campus, FL, U.S.; **Nilüfer Ertürkmen**, Ege University, Turkey; **Sue Fine**, Ras Al Khaimah Women's College (HCT), U.A.E.; **Amina Al Hashami**, Nizwa College of Applied Sciences, Oman; **Stephan Johnson**, Nagoya Shoka Daigaku, Japan; **Sean Kim**, Avalon, South Korea; **Gregory King**, Chubu Daigaku, Japan; **Seran Küçük**, Maltepe University, Turkey; **Jonee De Leon**, VUS, Vietnam; **Carol Lowther**, Palomar College, CA, U.S.; **Erin Harris-MacLead**, St. Mary's University, NS, Canada; **Angela Nagy**, Maltepe University, Turkey; **Huynh Thi Ai Nguyen**, Vietnam; **Daniel L. Paller**, Kinjo Gakuin University, Japan; **Jangyo Parsons**, Kookmin University, South Korea; **Laila Al Qadhi**, Kuwait University, Kuwait; **Josh Rosenberger**, English Language Institute University of Montana, MT, U.S.; **Nancy Schoenfeld**, Kuwait University, Kuwait; **Jenay Seymour**, Hongik University, South Korea; **Moon-young Son**, South Korea; **Matthew Taylor**, Kinjo Gakuin Daigaku, Japan; **Burcu Tezcan-Unal**, Zayed University, U.A.E.; **Troy Tucker**, Edison State College-Lee Campus, FL, U.S.; **Kris Vicca**, Feng Chia University, Taichung; **Jisook Woo**, Incheon University, South Korea; **Dunya Yenidunya**, Ege University, Turkey

**UNITED STATES** Mary Ahlman, Coastline Community College, Westminster, CA; **Marcarena Aguilar**, North Harris College, TX; **Rebecca Andrade**, California State University North Ridge, CA; **Lesley Andrews**, Boston University, MA; **Deborah Anholt**, Lewis and Clark College, OR; **Robert Anzelde**, Oakton Community College, IL; **Arlys Arnold**, University of Minnesota, MN; **Marcia Arthur**, Renton Technical College, WA; **Renee Ashmeade**, Passaic County Community College, NJ; **Anne Bachmann**, Clackamas Community College, OR; **Lida Baker**, UCLA, CA; **Ron Balsamo**, Santa Rosa Junior College, CA; **Lori Barkley**, Portland State University, OR; **Eileen Barlow**, SUNY Albany, NY; **Sue Bartch**, Cuyahoga Community College, OH; **Lora Bates**, Oakton High School, VA; **Barbara Batra**, Nassau County Community College, NY; **Nancy Baum**, University of Texas at Arlington, TX; **Rebecca Beck**, Irvine Valley College, CA; **Leslie Bennett**, UCLA, CA; **Linda Berendsen**, Oakton Community College, IL; **Jennifer Binckes Lee**, Howard Community College, MD; **Grace Bishop**, Houston Community College, TX; **Jean W. Bodman**, Union County College, NJ; **Virginia Bouchard**, George Mason University, VA; **Kimberley Briesch Sumner**, University of Southern California, CA; **Kevin Brown**, University of California, Irvine, CA; **Laura Brown**, Glendale Community College, CA; **Britta Burton**, Mission College, CA; **Allison L. Callahan**, Harold Washington College, IL; **Gabriela Cambiasso**, Harold Washington College, IL; **Jackie Campbell**, Capistrano Unified School District, CA; **Adele C. Camus**, George Mason University, VA; **Laura Chason**, Savannah College, GA; **Kerry Linder Catana**, Language Studies International, NY; **An Cheng**, Oklahoma State University, OK; **Carole Collins**, North Hampton Community College, PA; **Betty R. Compton**, Intercultural Communications College, HI; **Pamela Couch**, Boston University, MA; **Fernanda Crowe**, Intrax International Institute, CA; **Vicki Curtis**, Santa Cruz, CA; **Margo Czinski**, Washtenaw Community College, MI; **David Dahnke**, Lone Star College, TX; **Gillian M. Dale**, CA; **L. Dalgish**, Concordia College, MN; **Christopher Davis**, John Jay College, NY; **Sherry Davis**, Irvine University, CA; **Natalia de Cuba**, Nassau County Community College, NY; **Sonia Delgadillo**, Sierra College, CA; **Esmeralda Diriye**, Cypress College & Cal Poly, CA; **Marta O. Dmytrenko-Ahrabian**, Wayne State University, MI; **Javier Dominguez**, Central High School, SC; **Jo Ellen Downey-Greer**, Lansing Community College, MI; **Jennifer Duclos**, Boston University, MA; **Yvonne Duncan**, City College of San Francisco, CA; **Paul Dydman**, USC Language Academy, CA; **Anna Eddy**, University of Michigan-Flint, MI; **Zohan El-Gamal**, Glendale Community College, CA; **Jennie Farnell**, University of Connecticut, CT; **Susan Fedors**, Howard Community College, MD; **Valerie Fiechter**, Mission College, CA; **Ashley Fifer**, Nassau County Community College, NY; **Matthew Florence**, Intrax International Institute, CA; **Kathleen Flynn**, Glendale College, CA; **Elizabeth Fonsea**, Nassau County Community College, NY; **Eve Fonseca**, St. Louis Community College, MO; **Elizabeth Foss**, Washtenaw Community College, MI; **Duff C. Galda**, Pima Community College, AZ; **Christiane Galvani**, Houston Community College, TX; **Gretchen Gerber**, Howard Community College, MD; **Ray Gonzalez**, Montgomery College, MD; **Janet Goodwin**, University of California, Los Angeles, CA; **Alyona Gorokhova**, Grossmont College, CA; **John Graney**, Santa Fe College, FL; **Kathleen Green**, Central High School, AZ; **Nancy Hamadou**, Pima Community College-West Campus, AZ; **Webb Hamilton**, De Anza College, San Jose City College, CA; **Janet Harclerode**, Santa Monica Community College, CA; **Sandra Hartmann**, Language and Culture Center, TX; **Kathy Haven**, Mission College, CA; **Roberta Hendrick**, Cuyahoga Community College, OH; **Ginny Heringer**, Pasadena City College, CA; **Adam Henricksen**, University of Maryland, MD; **Carolyn Ho**, Lone Star College-CyFair, TX; **Peter Hoffman**, LaGuardia Community College, NY; **Linda Holden**, College of Lake County, IL; **Jana Holt**, Lake Washington Technical College, WA; **Antonio Iccarino**, Boston University, MA; **Gail Ibele**, University of Wisconsin, WI; **Nina Ito**, American Language Institute, CSU Long Beach, CA; **Linda Jensen**, UCLA, CA; **Lisa Jurkowitz**, Pima Community College, CA; **Mandy Kama**, Georgetown University, Washington, DC; **Stephanie Kasuboski**, Cuyahoga Community College, OH; **Chigusa Katoku**, Mission College, CA; **Sandra Kawamura**, Sacramento City College, CA; **Gail Kellersberger**, University of Houston-Downtown, TX; **Jane Kelly**, Durham Technical Community College, NC; **Maryanne Kildare**, Nassau County Community College, NY; **Julie Park Kim**, George Mason University, VA; **Kindra Kinyon**, Los Angeles Trade-Technical College, CA; **Matt Kline**, El Camino College, CA; **Lisa Kovacs-Morgan**, University of California, San Diego, CA; **Claudia Kupiec**, DePaul University, IL; **Renee La Rue**, Lone Star College-Montgomery, TX; **Janet Langon**, Glendale College, CA; **Lawrence Lawson**, Palomar College, CA; **Rachele Lawton**, The Community College of Baltimore County, MD; **Alice Lee**, Richland College, TX; **Esther S. Lee**, CSUF & Mt. SAC, CA; **Cherie Lenz-Hackett**, University of Washington, WA; **Joy Leventhal**, Cuyahoga Community College, OH; **Alice Lin**, UCI Extension, CA; **Monica Lopez**, Cerritos College, CA; **Dustin Lovell**, FLS International Marymount College, CA; **Carol Lowther**, Palomar College, CA; **Candace Lynch-Thompson**, North Orange County Community College District, CA; **Thi Thi Ma**, City College of San Francisco, CA; **Steve Mac Isaac**, USC Long Academy, CA; **Denise Maduli-Williams**, City College of San Francisco, CA; **Eileen Mahoney**, Camelback High School, AZ; **Naomi Mardock**, MCC-Omaha, NE; **Brigitte Maronde**, Harold Washington College, IL; **Marilyn Marquis**, Laposita College CA; **Doris Martin**, Glendale Community College; Pasadena City College, CA; **Keith Maurice**, University of Texas at Arlington, TX; **Nancy Mayer**, University of Missouri-St. Louis, MO; **Aziah McNamara**, Kansas State University, KS; **Billie McQuillan**, Education Heights, MN; **Karen Merritt**, Glendale Union High School District, AZ; **Holly Milkowart**, Johnson County Community College, KS; **Eric Moyer**, Intrax International Institute, CA; **Gino Muzzatti**, Santa Rosa Junior College, CA; **Sandra Navarro**, Glendale Community College, CA; **Melissa Nichelson**, Pasadena City College, CA; **Than Nyeinkhin**, ELAC, PCC, CA; **William Nedrow**, Triton College, IL; **Eric Nelson**, University of Minnesota, MN; **Than Nyeinkhin**, ELAC, PCC, CA; **Fernanda Ortiz**, Center for English as a Second Language at the University of Arizona, AZ; **Rhony Ory**, Ygnacio Valley High School, CA; **Paul Parent**, Montgomery College, MD; **Dr. Sumeeta Patnaik**, Marshall University, WV; **Oscar Pedroso**, Miami Dade College, FL; **Robin Persiani**, Sierra College, CA; **Patricia Prenz-Belkin**, Hostos Community College, NY; **Suzanne Powell**, University of Louisville, KY;

UNIT **1**

Marketing

READING ▶ identifying the main idea of a paragraph
VOCABULARY ▶ word families
WRITING ▶ writing a descriptive paragraph
GRAMMAR ▶ present continuous

**UNIT QUESTION**

# Why does something become popular?

**A** Discuss these questions with your classmates.

1. Do you and your friends like the same things? Do you wear the same clothes? Why do you think that is?

2. Look at the photo. Where are these people? What makes a place like this popular?

UNIT ▶▶▶▶
OBJECTIVE

Read the articles. Gather information and ideas to write a descriptive paragraph about a current trend and why it is popular.

**B** Listen to *The Q Classroom* online. Then answer these questions.

1. Yuna thinks that popularity grows by word of mouth. Do you think that is true?

2. What is an example of another reason that something becomes popular?

iQ ONLINE **C** Go online to watch the video about how stores try to encourage customers to buy things. Then check your comprehension.

VIDEO VOCABULARY

**invade** *(v.)* to enter a country in large numbers

**match** *(v.)* to have the same color or pattern as something else

**spread** *(v.)* to make something affect a bigger group of people

**stacks** *(n.)* neat piles of something

iQ ONLINE **D** Go to the Online Discussion Board to discuss the Unit Question with your classmates.

**E** Here are three different ways that something can become popular. Work with a partner. Complete the diagram with two advantages and two disadvantages for each.

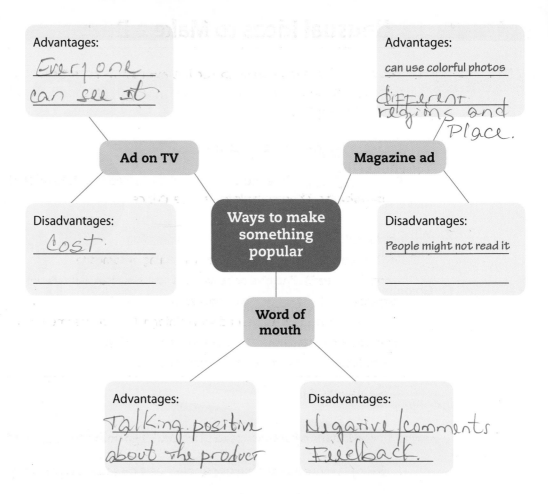

Advantages:

*Everyone can see it*

**Ad on TV**

Disadvantages:

*Cost.*

Advantages:

can use colorful photos

*different religions and Place.*

**Magazine ad**

Disadvantages:

People might not read it

**Ways to make something popular**

**Word of mouth**

Advantages:

*Talking positive about the product*

Disadvantages:

*Negative/comments Feedback.*

**F** Discuss these questions in a group.

1. What are some things that are popular among your classmates? How did you first learn about these things?

2. What is something that is popular now but wasn't popular last year?

# READING

## READING 1 | Unusual Ideas to Make a Buzz

 You are going to read an online article about how advertisers try to make things popular. Use the reading to gather information and ideas for your Unit Assignment.

## PREVIEW THE READING

**A.** **VOCABULARY** Here are some words from Reading 1. Read their definitions. Then complete each sentence.

> **clear** (*adjective*) 🔑 easy to see, hear, or understand
> **connect** (*verb*) 🔑 to join or to link to something or someone
> **contribute** (*verb*) 🔑 to give or be a part of something with other people
> **express** (*verb*) 🔑 to say or show how you think or feel
> **find out** (*phrasal verb*) to get or discover information about something
> **spread** (*verb*) 🔑 to affect a large area or group of people
> **trend** (*noun*) 🔑 a change to something different

🔑 Oxford 3000™ words

1. I don't know what time the mall opens. I'll go online to _____ find out _____.

2. Many Americans are buying smaller cars that use less gas. They are part of a _____ trend _____ that started a few years ago.

3. A small fire can _____ spread _____ quickly in a dry place.

4. Each member of the group should _____ contribute _____ equally to the project.

5. Thanks to the Internet, Jean can always _____ connect _____ with her family, even though they live far away.

6. Because Doug and Liz don't speak Spanish well, they couldn't _____ express _____ themselves well when on vacation in Spain.

7. It was very _____ clear _____ that Noriko didn't do her homework. She didn't know any answers during the class discussion.

**B.** Go online for more practice with the vocabulary.

**C.** PREVIEW Read the title and look at the pictures in the article about advertising. What do you think the article will say about advertising?

**D.** QUICK WRITE Why do you think that certain ideas or products become popular? Write three sentences. Include at least one example. Be sure to use this section for your Unit Assignment.

## WORK WITH THE READING

**A.** Read the article and gather information about why something becomes popular.

# Unusual Ideas to Make a Buzz

1    Every year companies spend millions of dollars on advertising to create buzz about their products—in other words, to get people talking about them. Companies know that people like to talk about unusual, funny, and remarkable things. Nowadays, companies are using many creative ways to help products become more popular.

2    One idea that can **contribute** to popularity is to do something very unusual. Red Bull™ is a company that makes energy drinks. They want people to feel energetic when they think about Red Bull™. So they sponsored an unusual event: 43-year-old Felix Baumgartner jumped from 39 kilometers up in space to set a new world record for skydiving. He traveled more than 1,300 kilometers per hour in a space suit with Red Bull™'s name on it. This is part of a new **trend** in advertising, in which companies pay for unusual events, hoping that customers will talk more about their products.

3    Some other companies choose to do something surprising so that people will remember their product and **spread** their idea. A good example is a company called Blendtec™. Tom Dickson, Blendtec™'s owner, had an idea to make his blenders look more interesting. He made videos showing his blenders mixing up unusual things. He put items like smartphones, rakes, or sports equipment into one of the machines and asked, "Will it blend?" People were surprised to see a blender cut a smartphone into small pieces. Everyone talked about the videos and wanted to **find out** more about the blenders. Dickson was invited to demonstrate his products on TV shows. His blenders became much more popular, and he sold a lot more of them.

**Felix Baumgartner sky-diving from space**

4 The company that makes Doritos™, a snack food, had a different idea about creating buzz. They decided to get their customers involved. So they began a competition. They asked customers to make their own TV ads. Then, they asked viewers to choose the ads that they liked the best. This created buzz because people like to participate and **express** their own opinions.

a rake in a Blendtec™ blender

5 Another way to make a product popular is to **connect** it in people's minds with something that they see often. To improve sales, the maker of Kit Kat™ chocolate bars used advertisements that connected Kit Kat™ bars with coffee. They hoped that every time people drank coffee, they would think of Kit Kat™ bars. They were right. Sales improved by more than 50 percent when people connected Kit Kat™ bars with coffee.

6 There are many ways that advertisers hope to make their products become popular: doing something surprising or exciting, asking customers to get involved, or connecting the product with something that people see regularly. Whatever method is used, the result is **clear**: more buzz and more popularity.

**B.** Match each product to the type of advertising used for it.

_c_ 1. Red Bull™          a. asked customers to make TV ads

_d_ 2. Blendtec™          b. connected the product with coffee

_a_ 3. Doritos™           c. used a skydiver

_b_ 4. Kit Kat™ bars      d. used their product to cut things to pieces

**C.** Write the correct paragraph number next to each idea from the reading. Then underline the sentence where you found the answer.

_4_ a. People like to participate and express their own opinions.

_3_ b. Sometimes companies do surprising things to get people talking about a product.

_1_ c. Advertisers try to create a buzz about their products.

_6_ d. There are many ways that advertisers try to make their products popular.

_2_ e. Some companies like to hold unusual events.

_3_ f. When people are surprised, they may talk about what they have seen.

**D.** Answer the questions. Then circle the answer in the reading.

1. What does the word *buzz* mean?

   People talk about it to make it popular.

2. How high was Felix Baumgartner when he jumped from space?

   39 kilometers

3. How fast did Felix Baumgartner travel on his skydiving adventure?

   1,300 kilometers per hour.

4. What items did Tom Dickson put in his blenders?

   smartphone, rake, sports equipment

5. What method did Kit Kat™ use to get people to buy more candy?

   connected with coffee

6. By how much did Kit Kat™ sales improve?

   more than 50%

7. Why do companies want to create buzz about their products?

   They will buy more products.

**E.** Complete each statement. Why did people talk about these products?

1. People talked about Red Bull™ because _____.

2. People talked about Blendtec™ because _____.

3. People thought about Doritos™ because _____.

4. People thought about Kit Kat™ because _____.

**iQ** ONLINE **F.** Go online to read *Predicting Future Trends* and check your comprehension.

## Q? WRITE WHAT YOU THINK

**A.** Discuss these questions in a group.

1. Which type of advertising from the reading do you think is most successful?

2. What is an advertisement that you can remember? Why do you remember it?

**B.** Choose one question from Activity A and write a response. Look back at your Quick Write on page 6 as you think about what you learned.

Question:_____

My Response: _____

_____

_____

## Reading Skill    Identifying the main idea of a paragraph

A **paragraph** is a group of sentences about one topic. The **main idea** of a paragraph is the most important point about the topic. You can often find the main idea in the first or second sentence of a paragraph. This is the **topic sentence**. The other sentences help explain or support the main idea. Identifying the main idea of a paragraph will help you to understand and remember what you read.

**A.** Read the paragraphs. Then circle the main ideas.

1.    (Experts often influence our actions and purchases.) For example, a doctor on a TV health show may recommend a medication. Because the doctor is an expert in healthcare, we expect her to be very knowledgeable about what medicines are best. We are more likely to follow her advice.

2.    (Other consumers also influence ~~Topic~~ our purchases.) When a consumer uses a product, we listen to his or her opinion. On the Internet, consumers can write their opinions about products. For example, on some travel websites, people write reviews of hotels and restaurants. Online bookstores share reviews from ordinary people. These websites are very popular because they show that people are interested in consumers' opinions.

**B.** Read the questions. Look back at Reading 1 on pages 6–7. Circle the correct answer for each question. Then write the key sentence from Reading 1 that helped you find the answer.

1.  What is the main idea of paragraph 2?
    a.  Felix Baumgartner set a new world record for skydiving from space.
    b.  Drinking Red Bull™ may give you more energy.
    c.  More companies are using unusual events to make people excited about their products.
        Key sentence: _____

2. What is the main idea of paragraph 3?
   a. People will spread your idea if it is surprising.
   b. Blentec™'s blenders are very powerful; they can chop up anything.
   c. Tom Dickson had a good idea.
      Key sentence: _____

3. What is the main idea of paragraph 4?
   a. The company that makes Doritos™ started a competition.
   b. People could make their own TV ads.
   c. Doritos™ customers participated, so they felt more involved.
      Key sentence: _____

4. What is the main idea of paragraph 5?
   a. The company used advertisement to connect Kit Kat™ bars with coffee.
   b. Connecting a product with something that people see often can help make it popular.
   c. The company hoped that sales would increase.
      Key sentence: _____

 **C.** Go online for more practice with identifying the main idea of a paragraph.

# READING 2 | How Do You Decide?

 You are going to read an article from a business magazine about who influences our shopping choices. Use the article to gather information and ideas for your Unit Assignment.

## PREVIEW THE READING

**A.** **VOCABULARY** Here are some words from Reading 1. Read the sentences. Circle the phrase that best matches the meaning of each underlined word.

1. Jordan's parents <u>influenced</u> his decision to apply to the college where they had studied.    *Verb*
   a. had an effect on
   b. postponed or delayed

2. I love to talk with people and solve their problems. I would like to be a <u>psychologist</u>.    *Noun*
   a. a person who knows what other people are thinking
   b. a person who studies the human mind

🔑 Oxford 3000™ words

3. When I got home from the mall, I showed my new <u>purchase</u> to my brother.
   *Nouns*
   a. a large box
   b. something that I bought

4. I highly <u>recommend</u> this book. It is a fascinating story.
   *Verb*
   a. say that something is good
   b. say what something is about

5. The <u>researcher</u> looked at how often TV stations schedule children's programs.
   *Nouns*
   a. person who studies something
   b. person who manages something

6. The <u>review</u> of the new TV show was very good.
   *Nouns*
   a. an article that judges a show and tells if it is good
   b. an article that tells the story of a show

7. Alan is very popular and has an active <u>social</u> life.
   *Adj.*
   a. related to being in school and studying cultures
   b. related to meeting people and spending time with them

8. The scientists did an unusual <u>study</u> about the behavior of mice.
   *Nouns*
   a. college course
   b. research project

iQ **ONLINE**   **B.** Go online for more practice with the vocabulary.

**C.** **PREVIEW** What do you think the article will say? Check (✓) your answer.

☑ People make their shopping choices because of what other people buy.

☐ People make their shopping choices because of what they like themselves.

**D.** **QUICK WRITE** Have you ever done something because all of your friends were doing it, too? What did you do? Did you enjoy it? Write your responses to the questions before you read the article. Be sure to use this section for your Unit Assignment.

# WORK WITH THE READING

◉ **A.** Read the article and gather information about why something becomes popular.

# How Do You Decide?

1    How do you decide what clothing or book to buy or which restaurant to eat at? You may think that you decide for yourself. But according to **studies** of human behavior, people around us greatly **influence** our choices and decisions.

2    **Psychologists** say that "**social** proof" influences us. Social proof is how other people's actions influence us. When we are not sure what to do, we look at what others are doing. The actions of other people are the "proof[1]" of the right thing to do. One example of this is a sidewalk experiment. If you stand still on a busy sidewalk and look up into the sky, no one will copy your actions. As one person, you probably won't influence other strangers. But social **researchers** discovered something interesting in New York City. When a group of four people looked up at the sky on a busy sidewalk, 80% of the passersby[2] looked up at the sky. The passersby thought the four people must know something special. A group of people influences the behavior of others.

3    Businesses are very interested in understanding social proof. They want to influence us to buy their products. For that reason, social proof is very important in advertising. Four groups of people give social proof: experts[3], other consumers[4], crowds, and friends. First, experts often influence our actions and **purchases**. For example, an expert on a TV health show may **recommend** a medicine. Because the expert is knowledgeable, we may follow the advice. Advertisers use experts for social proof.

4    Other consumers also influence our purchases and show social proof. When a consumer uses a product, we listen to his or her opinion. On the Internet, consumers can express their opinions about products. For example, people write **reviews** of hotels and restaurants on travel websites. Online bookstores have book reviews from ordinary people. These websites are very popular because people are interested in consumers' opinions.

5    The third type of social proof comes from crowds. McDonald's, the fast food giant, has a sign on every restaurant, "Billions and Billions Served." The crowds of people who eat at McDonald's are the social proof of McDonald's popularity. In a recent experiment, a major hotel company wanted to decrease the number of towels it washed. The first hotel room sign said "Help us help the environment. Please reuse your bath towel." Not many people did. The hotel

---

[1] **proof:** facts that show something is true
[2] **passersby:** people who are walking by a place

[3] **experts:** people who know a lot about something
[4] **consumers:** people who buy things or use services

changed the sign to say, "Most guests in this hotel reuse their towels. Will you?" 26% of the guests then reused their towels. Finally, they changed the sign to say, "Most guests in this room reuse their towels. Will you?" 33% reused their towels. In this case, the actions of a group influenced other people. According to another study, when a restaurant marks certain dishes as "Our most popular," sales of those dishes increase by at least 13%. The behavior of other people can influence actions and purchases.

6  Finally, there is the social proof of friends. Friends influence us the most — more than experts, crowds, or other consumers. Our friends are usually more like us than other people, and we trust their recommendations. A quick text message or smartphone photo can show a new purchase. That is perhaps the best advertising of all, and for companies, it is free. It is simply

friends talking about purchases. The next time you buy something, think about how you decided to buy it. It was probably a friend's influence!

**B.** Circle the correct answer for each question.

1. What is the main idea of the reading?
   - ⓐ Different groups of people influence our purchases.
   - b. Advertisers want to influence consumers.
   - c. One example of social proof is experts talking about medicines on TV.

2. What is the main idea of paragraph 2?
   - a. The sidewalk experiment shows that people are not influenced by an individual.
   - ⓑ The actions of other people will influence a person's behavior.
   - c. Psychologists in New York City studied social proof.

**C.** Answer the questions.

1. What is social proof?

   *Other people's actions influence us.*

2. Why are businesses interested in social proof?

   *They want to influence us to buy their products.*

3. Why do people follow the advice of experts?

   *Because the expert is knowledgeable*

4. Why are travel and book-review websites popular?

*Because people are interested iin consumers opinions*

5. What is probably the best advertising of all?

*Friends recommendationase.*

Critical Thinking **Tip**

Activity D asks you to put the sentences **in order** (what happens first, second, third, and so on). **Ordering** is one way to show you understand the ideas in a reading.

**D. Number the sentences in the order in which the ideas appear in the reading.**

*4* a.  Consumer reviews are an example of social proof.

*5* b.  Friends are the strongest social proof.

*1* c.  In social proof, others' actions influence our behavior.

*3* d.  Advertisers use experts to influence our purchases.

*2* e.  The actions of groups of people influence us to act the same way.

**E.  Complete the paragraph with words from the box.**

| advertising | consumers | friends | recommendations |
|---|---|---|---|
| behavior | experts | influence | |

Social proof is how other people's actions *influence* us.

A group of people can influence the *behavior* of others.

*experts* can influence our actions and purchases because

they are knowledgeable. We also sometimes buy things because of other

*consumers*, even if we don't know them. But the people who

influence us most are our *friends* because we trust their

*recomendation*. That may be the best *advertising* of all.

**F.  According to the magazine article, which of the following are examples of social proof? Check (✓) the boxes.**

☑ 1.  doing something because other people are doing it

☐ 2.  buying something because of a magazine ad

☑ 3.  staying at a hotel because of a review on a travel website

☑ 4.  sharing a text message about a recent purchase

☐ 5.  making a customer-produced video of a product

☑ 6.  following the advice of an expert

☐ 7.  watching a skydiver break a world record

# WRITE WHAT YOU THINK

**A.** Discuss the questions in a group. Look back at your Quick Write on page 11 as you think about what you learned.

1. Describe a time when you did something because of social proof.

2. Why do you think social proof is effective?

**B.** Think about the unit video, Reading 1, and Reading 2 as you discuss these questions. Then choose one question and write a response.

1. In what ways do companies use social proof to encourage you to buy new products?

2. How do new trends begin? Give an example of a new trend. Why did it become popular?

---

**Vocabulary Skill** | **Word families**

Learning about **word families** can help you improve your vocabulary. Word families are groups of words that come from the same root. If you know the meaning of the *noun form* of a word, you may also recognize the *verb form*.

In some word families, the noun form and the verb form are the same.

His teacher had a strong **influence** on him.      Parents **influence** their children.

noun                                                verb

---

**Tip for Success**

To help you determine if a word is a noun or a verb, remember that a noun is a person, place, or object, and a verb usually shows action.

**A.** Look at the pairs of words. Decide if each word is a noun or a verb. Then write the words in the correct side of the chart. Use a dictionary to help you.

| | | |
|---|---|---|
| ~~choice/choose~~ | discuss/discussion | inform/information |
| connect/connection | enjoy/enjoyment | thought/think |
| contribution/contribute | gift/give | |

| Nouns | Verbs |
|---|---|
| *choice* | *choose* |
| connection | connect          Inform |
| contribution | contribute        Think |
| discussion | discuss |
| enjoyment | enjoy |
| gift | give |
| information | |
| thought | |

**B. Read the sentences. Write N (noun) or V (verb) for each bold word.**

_V_ 1. My brothers **study** in the kitchen every night.

_N_ 2. The **study** showed important changes in trends.

_V_ 3. Steven wanted to **comment** on Lilly's presentation.

_N_ 4. I saw the **comment** Penny wrote on the website.

_N_ 5. My grandparents had an important **influence** on me.

_V_ 6. My friends often **influence** my book choices.

_N_ 7. Dr. Lee's **research** on weather is very interesting.

_V_ 8. Tom will **research** many colleges before making a decision.

_V_ 9. It is helpful to **review** your notes before a test.

_N_ 10. After I read the movie **review**, I didn't want to see the movie.

**C. Complete each sentence with a noun or a verb from activity B. For verbs, use the correct form of the simple present.**

1. Don _____studies_____ in the library at night.

2. Faisal usually ___reviews___ books for the college newspaper.

3. The weather has a strong ___influence___ on farmers' fruits and vegetables.

4. Ramona always ___comments___ on my clothing.

5. Carol ___researches___ news stories for her job at a magazine.

6. Allen's ___study___ is on the psychology of teenage shoppers.

7. There are only a few ___comment___ from my teacher on my essay.

8. TV commercials often ___influence___ our decisions about which products to buy.

**D. Go online for more practice with word families.**

# WRITING

 At the end of this unit, you will write a paragraph that describes a trend and explains why it is popular. This paragraph will include specific information from the readings and your own ideas.

| Writing Skill | Writing a descriptive paragraph |
| --- | --- |

When you write a **descriptive paragraph**, you give the reader information about your topic. The following are important elements in a descriptive paragraph.

- A *topic sentence* introduces what you are going to describe. The topic sentence introduces the *topic* or subject of the paragraph. It also gives the *controlling idea*, which is what you want to say about the topic.

  | topic | controlling idea |
  | --- | --- |

  Exciting events are one way for companies to gain interest in their products.
  Word of mouth is a useful and inexpensive way to advertise.

- In a descriptive paragraph, your **supporting sentences** help the reader understand the topic. They use descriptive words, such as adjectives and details to create a clear picture of your topic.

  Felix Baumgartner's jump from space was very **exciting**.
  He traveled **more than 1,300 kilometers per hour in a space suit with Red Bull's name on it**.
  The Blendtec video suddenly became **extremely popular** online.
  People were surprised to see a blender **cut a smartphone into small pieces**.

- A **concluding sentence** summarizes your ideas.

  Because many people saw the video of Baumgartner's jump, they connected Red Bull with excitement.
  The company sold more blenders because people were talking about their product.

**A. WRITING MODEL** Read the model paragraph below. Label the circled parts of the paragraph. Write *TS* (topic sentence), *SS* (supporting sentence), or *CS* (concluding sentence).

*TS* (Psychologists say that "social proof" influences us.) Social proof is how other people's actions influence us. When we are not sure what to do, we look at what others are doing. The actions of other people are the "proof" of the right thing to do. *SS* (One example of this is a sidewalk experiment.) If you stand still on a busy sidewalk and look up into the sky, no one will copy your actions. As one person, you probably won't influence other strangers. But social researchers discovered *SS* something interesting in New York City. (When a group of four people looked up at the sky on a busy sidewalk, 80 percent of the passersby looked up at the sky.) The passersby thought the four people must know something special. *CS* (A group of people influences the behavior of others.)

**B.** Match each part of the paragraph in Activity A with its purpose.

*b* 1. topic sentence a. summarizes your ideas

*c* 2. supporting sentences b. introduces what you will describe

*a* 3. concluding sentence c. help the reader understand the topic

**C.** Circle the topic sentence in this paragraph from Reading 2.

Finally, there is the social proof of friends. (Friends influence us the most—more than experts, crowds, or other consumers.) Our friends are usually more like us than other people, and we trust their recommendations. A quick text message or smartphone photo can show a new purchase. That is perhaps the best advertising of all, and for companies, it is free. It is simply friends talking about purchases. The next time you buy something, think about how you decided to buy it. It was probably a friend's influence!

**D.** Circle the best topic sentence for each group of sentences. Discuss your answers with a classmate. What is the topic? What is the controlling idea?

1. a. For example, torn jeans were popular years ago, but not now.
   b. The most popular clothing is not always popular the next year.
   c. I buy new clothes every year to be fashionable.

2. a. The computer lab is open from 9:00 until 2:00.
   b. For example, Brett doesn't have a computer at home.
   c. Classroom computers are very helpful for students.

3. (a.) Many older adults need a lesson on how to use a smartphone.
   b. My grandfather can't send a text message on his smartphone. _Detail_
   c. My grandmother keeps forgetting how to download apps.

4. (a.) Many new trends are actually old trends.
   b. TV game shows started over sixty years ago.
   c. Solar electricity was popular in the 1970s.

**E. Read the paragraphs. Then choose the best topic sentence.**

1. People of all ages are affected by this trend. Some people think that every job will require people to use some kind of technology. Some people even think that soon there will be computers that people actually wear as part of their clothing. Others think that these ideas will never happen. But there is no question that more and more, technology is a part of everyday life.

   a. It doesn't matter what your age is.
   (b.) Throughout the world, people are using more and more technology.
   c. Technology is getting smaller all the time.

2. Because of this, people from Africa to Australia are buying the same clothes, eating the same foods, and watching the same television shows. Some people are worried that people are losing parts of their history and culture and becoming more like people in other countries. In France, for example, there is a group that tries to be sure that there are enough TV shows that are made in France, not from other countries.

   a. Most people like the same things.
   (b.) Through the power of technology, people are becoming more similar all around the world.
   c. People are the same all over the world.

**F. WRITING MODEL** Read a student's model paragraph. Then write a topic sentence for the paragraph. Compare your topic sentence with a partner's.

---

_____

_____.

First of all, I usually don't like the new fashion trends. I have my own style. I usually buy well-made clothes, and I wear them for many years. Some of my clothes are more than five years old. Buying new clothes every year is very expensive. For example, trendy jeans cost over $100. I buy clothes that I like, not the latest trends.

---

**G.** Work with a partner. Complete the graphic organizer below. Write a topic sentence about something that is popular. Make sure your sentence contains a controlling idea. Then write two supporting ideas in the boxes. Your supporting ideas will help to describe your topic.

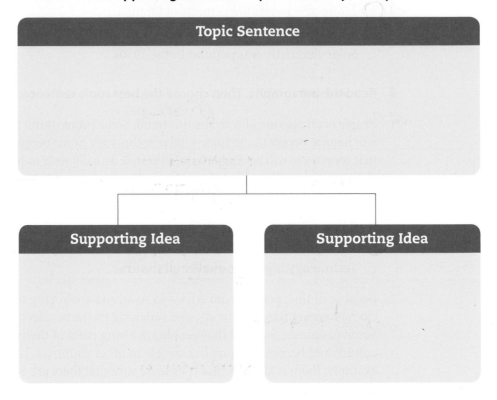

**H.** Take the ideas from Activity G and write a descriptive paragraph about the topic. Include a topic sentence, supporting sentences, and a concluding sentence.

**I.** Ask a classmate to read and comment on your writing. Use the peer-review checklist.

| | PEER-REVIEW CHECKLIST |
|---|---|
| ☐ | Does the paragraph have a topic sentence with a clear controlling idea? |
| ☐ | Do the ideas in the supporting sentences relate clearly to the topic? |
| ☐ | Do the supporting sentences use adjectives and details to help you understand the topic better? |
| ☐ | Does the paragraph have a clear conclusion? |

 **J.** Go online for more practice with descriptive paragraphs.

Use the **present continuous** to talk about activities in progress at the time of writing or that have started but not finished.

> Ramon **is talking** on the phone. He's **finding out** the arrival time. (activities in progress)
>
> We **are learning** about how ideas spread. (action started but not finished)
>
> The new trend **is contributing** to higher costs. (change in progress)

✳ Use the present continuous with words like *today, this week,* or time periods around the present.

> <u>This week</u> I **am studying** for exams.
>
> <u>These days</u>, more guests **are reusing** their towels in hotels.

To form the present continuous, use the verb *to be* and then the *–ing* form of the main verb.

If the verb ends in *e*, delete the *e* and add *–ing*.

> use → using      change → changing      lose → losing

Use the present continuous to talk about changes. For example, *changing, becoming, growing, increasing.*

> TV ads **are becoming** like short movies.
>
> The Internet **is changing** the way companies advertise.

Some verbs are not used with the present continuous. For example, *know, want, need, understand, like, love, believe, see, hear.*

> I **want** to go with you, but I'm studying right now.

**A.** Read the paragraph and circle verbs in the present continuous. Then answer the questions. Compare your answers with a partner.

1. Nowadays more and more companies are (making) advertisements that involve their customers. These companies (are using) many creative ways to help products become more popular. Researchers believe social proof is the idea behind this trend. This is because when we are not sure what to do, we look at what others (are doing.) More and more people (are using) smartphones and social media to share news about their purchases with their friends.

2. Why is the present continuous used in the first sentence?
   *Nowadays, more and more companies <u>are making</u> advertisements that involve their customers.*
   (a) The action happens all the time.
   b. The action is taking place at the time of writing.
   c. The action is completed.

3. Why is the present continuous **not** used in this sentence?
   *Researchers believe social proof is the idea behind this trend.*
   a. The action is happening now.
   b. The action is taking place at the time of writing.
   c. The verb *believe*, is not used in the present continuous.

**B.** **Complete each sentence with the present continuous of the word in parentheses. Remember to add the correct form of the verb *be*.**

1. Companies _are using_ (use) new ways of advertising to reach their customers.

2. Young people _are following_ (follow) new trends in fashion.

3. Teenagers _are copying_ (copy) their friends and doing the same things.

4. They _are buying_ (buy) the same clothing and the same devices.

5. Customers _are complaining_ (complain) that the advertisements are too boring.

6. Through online videos, Blendtec™ _is spreading_ (spread) the word about its products.

7. The company _is improving_ (improve) its reputation by using customers to share their ideas.

8. This month our store isn't advertising on the radio, so we _are losing_ (lose) some customers.

9. Maria doesn't wear the same thing twice. She _is is trying_ always (try) new clothes to see how they look.

10. I think you _are being_ (be) very silly about following new trends.

**C. Go online for more practice with the present continuous.**

**D. Go online for the grammar expansion.**

In this assignment, you will describe a trend that interests you and explain why this trend is popular. As you prepare your descriptive paragraph, think about the Unit Question, "Why does something become popular?" Use information from Reading 1, Reading 2, the unit video, and your work in this unit to support your paragraph. Refer to the Self-Assessment checklist on page 24.

Go to the Online Writing Tutor for a writing model and alternate Unit Assignments.

## PLAN AND WRITE

**Tip** for Success

When you brainstorm ideas before writing, think of as many ideas as you can. You don't need to use all of them. Just use the best ones.

**A. BRAINSTORM** Think about current trends. Write down as many ideas as you can. For example, you can list trends in cars, food, or technology.

_____

_____

_____

**B. PLAN** Choose one trend from your list in Activity A as your topic. Answer the questions. Then tell your partner about your topic.

1. What is the trend? Describe it.

_____

_____

2. Does the trend help people connect with others? How?

_____

_____

3. Why is the trend popular? What is new and different about it?

_____

_____

4. How did this trend start and spread or become popular?

_____

_____

**C.** **WRITE** Use your **PLAN** notes to write your descriptive paragraph. Go to *iQ Online* to use the Online Writing Tutor.

1. Write a topic sentence for your paragraph. Include your topic and your controlling idea in your sentence. Then use some of your answers from Activity B to write your paragraph.

2. Look at the Self-Assessment checklist to guide your writing.

## REVISE AND EDIT

**A.** **PEER REVIEW** Read your partner's paragraph. Then go online and use the Peer Review worksheet. Discuss the review with your partner.

**B.** **REWRITE** Based on your partner's review, revise and rewrite your paragraph.

Writing **Tip**

Read your paragraph more than once. For example, read once for ideas and to be sure you support your topic sentence. Read again to check your verb tenses.

**C.** **EDIT** Complete the Self-Assessment checklist as you prepare to write the final draft of your paragraph. Be prepared to hand in your work or discuss it in class.

| SELF-ASSESSMENT | | |
|:---:|:---:|:---|
| Yes | No | |
| ☐ | ☐ | Do all the sentences in the paragraph support your topic sentence? |
| ☐ | ☐ | Do you have a concluding sentence that summarizes your ideas? |
| ☐ | ☐ | Underline all of the verbs in the present continuous. Are they in the correct form? |
| ☐ | ☐ | Does your paragraph include vocabulary from the unit? |
| ☐ | ☐ | Did you check the paragraph for punctuation, spelling, and grammar? |

**D.** **REFLECT** Go to the Online Discussion Board to discuss these questions.

1. What is something new you learned in this unit?

2. Look back at the Unit Question—Why does something become popular? Is your answer different now than when you started the unit? If yes, how is it different? Why?

# TRACK YOUR SUCCESS

**Circle the words you have learned in this unit.**

**Nouns**
psychologist AWL
purchase 🔑 AWL
researcher AWL
review 🔑
study 🔑
trend 🔑 AWL

**Verbs**
connect 🔑
contribute 🔑 AWL
express 🔑
influence 🔑
recommend 🔑
spread 🔑

**Adjectives**
clear 🔑
social 🔑

**Phrasal Verbs**
find out

🔑 Oxford 3000™ words

AWL Academic Word List

**Check (✓) the skills you learned. If you need more work on a skill, refer to the page(s) in parentheses.**

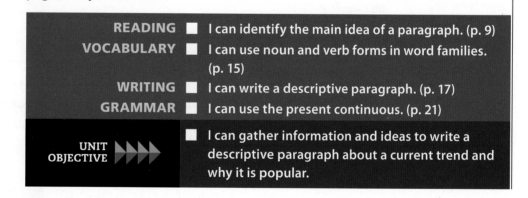

| | |
|---|---|
| **READING** ☐ | I can identify the main idea of a paragraph. (p. 9) |
| **VOCABULARY** ☐ | I can use noun and verb forms in word families. (p. 15) |
| **WRITING** ☐ | I can write a descriptive paragraph. (p. 17) |
| **GRAMMAR** ☐ | I can use the present continuous. (p. 21) |
| **UNIT OBJECTIVE** ▶▶▶▶ ☐ | I can gather information and ideas to write a descriptive paragraph about a current trend and why it is popular. |

**2**

READING ▶ getting meaning from context
VOCABULARY ▶ suffixes
WRITING ▶ brainstorming
GRAMMAR ▶ future with *will*

Psychology

**UNIT QUESTION**

# How do colors affect the way we feel?

**A** Discuss these questions with your classmates.

1. What's your favorite color? Why do you like it?

2. Imagine that you walk into a room that has yellow walls. How does that color make you feel?

3. Look at the photo. How do the colors of these houses affect this town?

**B** Listen to *The Q Classroom* online. Then answer these questions.

1. What colors did the students mention? How do the colors make the students feel?

2. What color would you like to paint your room? Why?

 **C** Go to the Online Discussion Board to discuss the Unit Question with your classmates.

**D** Look at the pictures and read the captions. Then discuss the questions with a partner.

1. What color is special for each person? Why?

2. Valeria McCullock likes the color blue. It makes her feel peaceful. She says that wearing blue makes her feel like she is in a dream all day. How does the color blue make you feel?

3. What colors do you like to wear? Why?

4. What colors do you not like to wear? Why?

**1** Valeria McCullock wears only blue. She says blue makes her feel peaceful. "Wearing blue for me is being in a dream all day," she says.

**2** Tom Le's favorite color is red. He says, "I like red because it's a warm, bright color. Red makes me feel happy."

**3** All of Stephin Merritt's clothes are brown. He says that it's easy to wear brown because all browns go together. Also, brown doesn't show dirt or stains. Merritt says, "I have brown hair and eyes, and I believe in matching."

**4** Elizabeth Sweetheart dresses in green. It makes her think of nature—trees, flowers, grass. "I missed nature when I moved to New York," she says.

## READING 1 | How Colors Make Us Think and Feel

**UNIT OBJECTIVE** ▶▶▶▶ You are going to read an article about colors and cultural differences. Use the article to gather information and ideas for your Unit Assignment.

# PREVIEW THE READING

**A. VOCABULARY** Here are some words from Reading 1. Read the sentences. Then write each <u>underlined</u> word next to the correct definition.

1. The weather can <u>affect</u> us. When it's cold and rainy, many people feel sad.

2. When Khalid came to Miami from Saudi Arabia, it was hard for him to understand some things about American <u>culture</u>. For example, he didn't understand why people wore jeans to nice restaurants.

3. You often know what <u>emotions</u> people are feeling even if they don't say anything. People cry when they are sad and smile or laugh when they are happy.

4. After Ana lost her job, she started having <u>psychological</u> problems. It was very stressful for her, so she worried a lot and felt very sad.

5. The doctor told Bettina to do some <u>specific</u> things to improve her health. He told her to exercise twice a week and to eat less junk food.

6. The color red has many meanings. It can <u>represent</u> danger, anger, or action.

7. Tom is <u>unaware</u> of how loudly he talks on his cell phone, so he keeps doing it.

8. It's a <u>universal</u> belief that friendship is important. I don't know anyone who doesn't think so.

a. _represent_ *(verb)* to be a picture, example, or sign of something

b. _affect_ *(verb)* to make someone or something change in a particular way; to influence someone or something

c. _emotions_ *(noun)* strong feelings such as fear or anger

d. _culture_ *(noun)* the ideas, beliefs, and ways of doing things in a particular society or country

e. _universal_ *(adjective)* involving everyone in the world or in a certain group

_don't know_

f. ___unaware___ *(adjective)* not knowing or noticing someone or something

g. ___psychological___ *(adjective)* connected with the mind or the way it works

h. ___specific___ *(adjective)* particular, not general

 **B.** Go online for more practice with the vocabulary.

**C.** **PREVIEW** Look at the headings, the color wheel, and the picture in Reading 1. Answer these questions.

1. How many sections are there? Which section is the painting on page 32 related to?

_____

2. Which section do you think will discuss different countries?

_____

3. On the color wheel, what are two warm colors? What are two cool colors?

_____

4. Look at the three words defined in the footnotes. Do you know any of these words already? Which ones?

_____

**D.** **QUICK WRITE** Think about the color red. Write a few sentences about how it makes you feel. If possible, give examples to support your answers. Be sure to use this section for your Unit Assignment.

# WORK WITH THE READING

**A.** Read the textbook article and gather information about how colors affect the way we feel.

## How Colors Make Us Think and Feel

What does the color pink make you think of?
How does the color blue make you feel?
Why do hospital doctors wear white coats?
What color room makes you feel relaxed?

### Colors affect everyone

1   Each person may have a different answer to these questions, but we can agree that colors **affect** everyone. We think carefully about color when we choose our clothes or select paint for a room. But we are often **unaware** of how color affects us. For example, the color of a room may affect our **emotions**. Advertisers use color to influence our choices at the supermarket. In addition, we may not realize that colors have many different meanings.

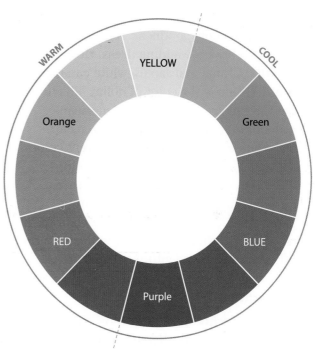

a color wheel

### Universal meaning

2   Colors in nature have **universal** meaning. For example, trees and plants are green, so the color green often **represents** life and nature. Blue, the color of the sky, oceans, and lakes, makes us think of air, water, and peace. Colors in the red spectrum[1]—yellow, orange, and red—are warm colors. Those colors may give us a feeling of warmth and comfort or feelings of anger. Colors in the blue spectrum—colors such as blue, green, and purple—are cool colors. They often give a feeling of calmness or sadness. These ideas about color are similar around the world.

### Colors in health

3   Humans have known about the power of color for a long time. Ancient **cultures** in China, Egypt, and India used colors to heal sicknesses. People believed that each color had a healing power. For example, people used blue to decrease pain. Even today, some people say that colors can help people feel better. However, research shows that although colors may change the way a person feels, they cannot heal an illness.

[1] **spectrum:** a group of colors

## Cultural meaning

4    Colors also have different meanings in different cultures. A color may represent good feelings in one culture but bad feelings in another. For example, in the United States, white represents goodness. It is usually the color of a bride's wedding dress. However, in India, China, and Japan, white can mean death. Green is the color of dollar bills in the U.S., so green may make Americans think of money. But in China, green can represent a loss of respect[2]. Different colors sometimes represent the same idea in different cultures. In European cultures, purple is the color of royalty for kings and queens. In Asia, yellow is the color of royalty. In addition, one color will have many different meanings within one culture.

**a Chinese emperor wearing yellow**

## Color psychology

5    Color **psychology** is the study of how colors affect our emotions. Researchers are finding that colors can change our behavior in **specific** ways. For example, one research study showed that people could lift heavy weights more easily in blue rooms. Other studies have looked at how colors influence decisions. Soccer referees made more decisions against teams that wore black uniforms. Tae kwon do[3] referees gave competitors in blue clothing higher scores than competitors in red. In another study, students who saw the color red before a test did much more poorly. Of course, these test results might vary from culture to culture.

6    Most people do not realize how much color affects them. It can affect how people think, feel, and act. Some colors, such as those in nature, can have the same meaning for everyone. Other colors' meanings may be different in different cultures. We can increase our understanding of ourselves and the world around us by learning about what colors can mean or represent.

---

[2] **respect:** the feeling that someone or something is important

[3] **tae kwon do:** a Korean art of self-defense using kicks

**B. Read the statements. Write *T* (true) or *F* (false). Then correct each false statement to make it true.**

_T_ 1. Most of us are unaware of how colors affect us.

_____

_F_ 2. Each color has only one meaning.

Color have many meanings.

_T_ 3. For people around the world, colors in nature have similar meanings.

_____

_T_ 4. In the past, some people believed that colors could heal people.

_____

_F_ 5. Research studies about color psychology show that color does not affect our actions or emotions.

Research shows that colors do affect our actions and emotion.

**C. Write what each color represents, according to the article. Give as many answers as possible.**

| Blue | Green | Red | Yellow | White |
|------|-------|-----|--------|-------|
| air | life | anger | warmth | goodness |
| sky | money | warm [adj] | royalty | death |
| ocean | nature. | comfort | comfort | peace. |
| water | loss of respect | danger | anger | |
| calmness | calmness | warmth (now) | | |
| sadness. | cool. | | | |

**D. Use the words to write sentences. Use information from the reading.**

1. United States / white  In the United States, white means goodness.

2. Ancient Egypt / colors _____

3. Japan / white _____

4. United States / green _____

5. China / green _____

6. Asia / yellow _____

7. Europe / purple _____

**E.** For each section of the article, write the main idea in your own words. Use some of the phrases from the box.

| | | |
|---|---|---|
| can affect | give a feeling of | may give us |
| can change | makes us think of | may represent |
| can have the same meaning | may be different | might vary |

1. Colors affect everyone _Although we may be unaware of it, colors can affect_

   _us and have different meanings._ _____

2. Universal meaning _____

   _____

3. Colors in health _____

   _____

4. Cultural meaning _____

   _____

5. Color psychology _____

   _____

# WRITE WHAT YOU THINK

**A.** Discuss these questions in a group. Then choose one question and write a response.

1. According to the article, soccer referees made more decisions against teams wearing black uniforms. Why do you think that happened?

2. Think about the color of your bedroom or living room. How does the color make you feel? Would you like to change the color? Why or why not?

**B.** Choose one of the questions and write a response. Look back at your Quick Write on page 30 as you think about what you learned.

## Reading Skill    Getting meaning from context

If you find a word you don't know in a text, you can use the **context** to help you understand the meaning of the word. The context is the other words near the unknown word.

context

It was a **joyful** celebration. Everyone was very happy.

context

The red sign told me that there was **danger** and some possibility of injury.

From the context, you can understand that the word *joyful* means "very happy." From the example, you can understand that *danger* means "a chance that someone might get hurt."

Critical Thinking **Tip**

In Activities A and B, you will use the context to understand the meaning of new words. Using context to guess meaning can help you read more fluently.

**A.** Read these sentences from Reading 1. Circle the words that give the context for the bold word in each sentence.

1. Those colors may give us a **feeling** of (warmth) and (comfort) or feelings of (anger).

2. Ancient cultures in China, Egypt, and India used colors to **heal** sicknesses. For example, people used blue to (decrease pain.)

3. In the United States, white represents goodness. It is usually the color of a **bride**'s (wedding dress.)

4. In European cultures, purple is the color of **royalty** for (kings and queens.)

5. Color **psychology** is the (study) of how colors affect our (emotions.)

6. Soccer **referees** made more (decisions) against (teams) that wore black uniforms.

**B.** Write a definition for each word from Activity A. Then check your definitions in your dictionary.

1. feeling      _emotion_
2. heal         _decrease pain_
3. bride        _A woman getting married_
4. royalty      _King, Queen, princess, price_
5. psychology   _Study of the mind and emotions_
6. referees     _People who make decision For Teams._

  **C.** Go online for more practice with getting meaning from context.

# READING 2 | The Importance of Color in Business

You are going to read an article about how colors can affect the way people think about companies. Use the article to gather information and ideas for your Unit Assignment.

## PREVIEW THE READING

**Vocabulary Skill Review**

In Unit 1, you learned about words that are both nouns and verbs. Look at the vocabulary in this activity. Which two vocabulary words are both nouns and verbs?

**A.** **VOCABULARY** Here are some words from Reading 2. Read the sentences. Circle the answer that best matches the meaning of each underlined word.

*NOUN*

1. Advertising in newspapers helped the restaurant increase its business.
   a. writing articles
   b. talking to customers
   c. telling people about products

2. Choosing a college is difficult. I have to carefully consider all my choices. *VERB*
   a. think about
   b. be worried about
   c. measure

3. My car is not very dependable. My battery died three times this month! *Sure, safe*   *Adverb*   *Confiable  Fuerte*
   a. important
   b. forceful
   c. reliable

4. I'm going to encourage Jorge to apply for the new job at the radio station. I think it's the perfect job for him.
   a. convince
   b. research
   c. command

5. Our family recycles paper and plastic to help protect the environment. *NOUN*
   a. machines
   b. natural world
   c. people

6. She left her job because she wants to establish her own company. *Verb*
   a. create
   b. sell
   c. research

7. A service that many hotels offer is helping with luggage. *NOUN*
   a. relationship between companies
   b. thing that a company does for you
   c. rule that a company follows

8. These new cell phones come in a variety of colors. I don't know which one to choose! *varayati*   *noun*
   a. large selection
   b. small choice
   c. very tiny group

**B.** Go online for more practice with the vocabulary.

**C.** **PREVIEW** Preview the article and circle the names of seven companies. Then discuss the companies with a partner. What do you know about these companies? What are their products or services?

Oxford 3000™ words

## WORK WITH THE READING

**A.** Read the magazine article and gather information about how color affects the way we feel.

# The Importance of Color in Business

1   If you walk into a McDonald's restaurant, what colors will you see? Probably yellow and red. And when you think about McDonald's, you will think about those two bright and cheerful colors. Every year large companies spend millions of dollars on **advertising**. They want you to buy their products and use their **services**, and they want you to remember their company name. Companies use color so that you will notice them and so that you will think about them when you see their colors. One research project showed that color helps people remember company names. Colors are very important to businesses.

2   Blue is often used by computer companies. IBM, Microsoft, and Dell all use the color blue to show that their companies are serious and **dependable**. Like the sky and the ocean, blue can be both peaceful and powerful. To show that their computers are for serious people, many companies used to make their computers black or gray. But Apple computer company decided that they wanted computers to be fun instead of serious. For that reason, they made their iMac computers in a **variety** of different colors in the late 1990s. Today, their computers, laptops, and cell phones come in a variety of colors.

3   BP uses green and yellow for its colors. It is the only large oil company to use green. Green is the color of nature. Yellow is the color of the sun. Both colors are bright and cheerful. BP hopes that people will think of it as a friendly company. In addition, green may make you think of the **environment**. BP wants people to think of it as a company that cares about the environment.

4   United Parcel Service (UPS) is a big delivery company. Its company color is brown. When UPS started in the 1920s, brown was a good color for a safe, reliable company. From the beginning, UPS used brown trucks and brown uniforms. In today's world, brown may seem like a boring color choice for a company. But UPS decided to make it a positive symbol of its business. Their ads ask, "What can brown do for you?" When people see the big brown UPS trucks, the company hopes they will think of excellent, dependable service.

5   All over the world, companies use color to **establish** their brand[1] and to **encourage** people to buy their products. Companies believe that customers respond strongly to their colors. It isn't surprising that companies carefully **consider** the colors for their products and their advertising.

**A UPS truck and delivery person**

[1] **brand:** the name of a product that is made by a specific company

**B. Check (✓) the main idea of the article.**

____ 1. Companies don't care if you remember their colors, as long as you buy their products.

✓ 2. Companies use color so you will notice them and remember their company when you see their colors.

____ 3. Blue is a good color for computer companies.

____ 4. Many companies use green because it shows they care about the environment.

**C. Complete the chart with information from the article.**

| Name of company | Company colors | Feelings that colors give |
| --- | --- | --- |
| McDonald's | red and yellow | bright, cheerful |
| Computer IBM, Microsoft, Dell | Blue | dependable, peaceful, powerful |
| Apple | variety of colors | Fun |
| BP | green and yellow | bright cheerful |
| UPS | brown | safe dependable |

**D. Write one or two sentences to describe each company, its colors, and the meaning of the colors. Use your answers from Activity C.**

1. McDonald's: _McDonald's uses red and yellow because they are bright and cheerful colors._

2. UPS: _UPS company use brown because They will think of excellent._

3. computer companies: _____

4. BP: _____

**E. Complete each statement with a word from the box. Use the context in the reading to help you understand each word.**

| cheerful | positive | products | reliable | respond |
| --- | --- | --- | --- | --- |

1. Red, yellow, and green are examples of _cheerful_ colors.

2. UPS wants customers to see them as a dependable company. In other words, customers should think UPS is _reliable_.

3. Some people think that brown is boring, which is negative. UPS has made brown a ___positive___ symbol.

4. Some of the ___products___ in the article are computers, cell phones, and oil.

5. When customers ___respond___ to a company's colors, they remember the brand and the products.

 **F. Go online to read *Men, Women, and Color* and check your comprehension.**

 ## WRITE WHAT YOU THINK

**A. Discuss the questions in a group. Look back at your Quick Write on page 37 as you think about what you learned.**

1. Choose three companies from Reading 2. Then note the color or colors that each company uses. Do you think that the colors they use influence how you think of them? Why or why not?

2. Imagine that you are designing a new restaurant. Decide what kind of restaurant it is. What colors would you use for the signs, the walls, the plates, and the napkins in the restaurant? Why?

 **B. Go online to watch the video about Pantone, a company that identifies and creates colors for companies. Then check your comprehension.**

| VIDEO VOCABULARY |
|---|
| **formula** (*n.*) a list of ingredients for making something |
| **shade** (*n.*) a type of a particular color |
| **signature** (*n.*) a particular quality that makes something different from other similar things and makes it easy to recognize |
| **standardize** (*v.*) to make things of a certain type the same as each other |

Writing **Tip**
When you describe a business and its colors, use the simple present. Also use the simple present to give your own opinion. Check that each sentence has a subject and a verb.

**C. Think about the unit video, Reading 1, and Reading 2 as you discuss these questions. Then choose one question and write a response.**

1. Think of a company or service that you are familiar with. What colors does it use for its products and advertising? Why do you think the company chose those colors?

2. Imagine that you are going to design a library room for children. What colors would you use for the tables and shelves, for the walls, and for a reading area? Why would you use those colors?

A **suffix** is a letter or group of letters at the end of a word. A suffix changes the form of a word. Common suffixes for changing a noun to an adjective are *–ful* and *–al*.

Nathaniel's favorite **color** is purple.
noun

Elizabeth loved to plant **colorful** flowers.
adjective

The researcher finished the **experiment** in one month.
noun

The tests were **experimental**, and they didn't prove anything.
adjective

Understanding suffixes can help you increase your vocabulary. If you know the meaning of a noun, then you may be able to also understand its adjective form.

| Noun | Adjective | Noun | Adjective |
| --- | --- | --- | --- |
| cheer | cheerful | education | educational |
| joy | joyful | nation | national |

Sometimes when you add a suffix, there are spelling changes to the noun form.

| Noun | Adjective | Noun | Adjective |
| --- | --- | --- | --- |
| biology | biological | finance | financial |

**A. Read each sentence. Write *N* (noun) or *ADJ* (adjective) for each bold word.**

__N__ 1.   Martin left his restaurant in his son's **care**.

__ADJ__ 2.   Laura was **careful** when she chose a company logo.

__ADJ__ 3.   The color green is a **universal** symbol of nature.

__N__ 4.   Kathryn feels small when she thinks about how big the **universe** is.

__N__ 5.   **Psychology** was Mary's favorite subject in college.

__ADJ__ 6.   The doctor was concerned about Alan's **psychological** problems.

__ADJ__ 7.   The president greeted the king with a **respectful** bow.

__N__ 8.   The new police officer quickly won the **respect** of the local residents.

**B.** Complete the chart with the correct form of each word. Then check your answers in the dictionary.

*[handwritten above Nouns column:]* psychology  *[handwritten above Adjectives column:]* psychological

| Nouns | Adjectives |
|---|---|
| 1. addition | additional |
| 2. emotion | *emotional* |
| 3. nature | *natural* |
| 4. *peace* | peaceful |
| 5. *person* *culture* *universe* | personal *cultural* *universal* |

**Tip** for Success

When you learn a new word, look in the dictionary for its other forms such as noun, verb, adjective, and adverb. This is an easy way to expand your vocabulary.

**C.** Complete the paragraph with a noun or adjective from Activity B.

Many people don't like running because they think it's difficult, but I really enjoy it. I usually run in a beautiful park near my house. There are lots of trees and birds in the park. I like running there because I like ___*nature*___ . The park is far

away from the noise of the city, so it's very quiet and
___*peaceful*___ . Some people prefer to run with
another ___*person*___ , but I prefer to run alone,
especially before work. My job is stressful, but running helps me feel more
relaxed. I think it's good for my physical and ___*emotimal*___ health. I
usually run three miles every morning, but sometimes I have time for a(n)
___*addition*___ mile or two. Maybe someday I'll run ten miles!

**iQ** ONLINE   **D.** Go online for more practice with suffixes.

**UNIT OBJECTIVE** ▶▶▶▶ At the end of this unit, you will write a proposal for a new business. In your proposal you will choose the colors for the business and explain why you chose these colors. This proposal will include specific information from the readings and your own ideas.

## Writing Skill    Brainstorming

**Brainstorming** is a way to get ideas before you write. When you brainstorm, you write down ideas quickly. Here are three useful ways to brainstorm.

**Listing** is a way to quickly write down ideas related to your topic. For example, if your topic is what the color white represents in your culture, you might write a quick list with ideas such as *goodness, cleanliness,* and *freshness.*

Making **idea maps** can also help you brainstorm. Write a key word in a center circle. Then write related words around the key word.

In **freewriting**, you give yourself five or ten minutes to write down all of your thoughts about a topic. Freewriting helps you think freely and creatively.

Here are some tips for brainstorming.

- Write down every idea that comes to you for five or ten minutes.
- Don't worry about whether an idea is a good one or not.
- Try to stay focused and write only about your topic.
- When you finish, look at your ideas. Choose the best ideas to develop for your writing.

**A.** Read the topic and questions below. Then list ideas that will help you with the topic.

*Topic:* Think of your favorite color. What items do you have in that color? Why do you like the color? How does it make you feel?

_____        _____

_____        _____

_____        _____

_____        _____

**B.** Read the topic below. Write each color in the center circle. Then add ideas around each color to make idea maps.

*Topic:* Think of a national flag. What are the main colors in the flag? What does each color represent?

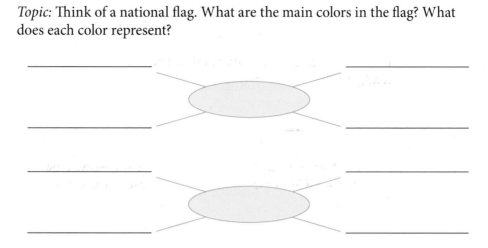

**C.** WRITING MODEL  Read the freewriting example. Cross out information that does not focus on the topic. Compare your answers with a partner.

**Topic:** How do companies use color to advertise their products? Write about companies that use color effectively.

*Companies and colors, Internet companies—Google uses lots of different colors, they are bright, happy colors—eBay also uses many different bright colors. Are they the same colors? My brother bought a bicycle on eBay. He rides it to work. Stores—Macy's department store uses red. I like the color red. It's a strong, exciting color. Macy's uses a red star in its advertisements. I always think of the red star and Macy's. Sometimes I shop at Macy's. The red star is a good symbol. It's easy to remember and recognize.*

**D.** Here's the beginning of a paragraph about the topic from Activity C. Underline information in Activity C that can be used in the paragraph.

Macy's and Target, two large department stores, both use the color red in their advertising.

**E.** Read the questions below. Then follow the steps to brainstorm and share your ideas.

*Topic:* Think of a well-known restaurant, clothing store, department store, or company. How does the company use color in their advertising or inside their place of business? How do the colors make you feel?

**Steps:**

1. First, choose a business to write about. Then brainstorm for five to ten minutes. Use listing, idea maps, or freewriting.

2. After you stop writing, read through your notes. Underline the ideas you want to use in your writing.

3. Share your brainstorming with your partner. Explain your ideas and answer any questions.

**F.** Write a paragraph about the topic. Use your brainstorming notes and any new ideas.

 **G.** Go online for more practice with brainstorming.

---

## Grammar | Future with *will*

In academic writing, use the future with *will* for predictions about the future and to express what experts predict.

> The designer **will establish** a second office in a new location.
> There **will be** a survey asking about the best color for the new library.

Note: You can soften a prediction by using *probably*. You can also use *may* instead of the future with *will*.

> The designer **will <u>probably</u> establish** a second office in a new location.
> The designer **<u>may</u> establish** a second office in a new location.

Use the future with *will* to make a promise.

> I **will help** you in about an hour.

Use the future with *will* to express plans in more formal writing.

> Next month we **will decide on** new colors for the kitchen.

Use the future with *will* to express a decision made at the moment of writing.

> **I'll go** to the meeting with you.

Note: Use the future with *be going to* to express a decision or plans that you made previously. This form is more common in informal speaking and writing.

> I **am going to have** dinner with my cousin.

**A. Complete the paragraphs with the future with *will*.**

Every year, the biggest paint companies introduce their newest "color of the year." Last week, companies announced their new colors, and designers are very excited about them. These wonderful new paints _will be_ available in January of next year.

    1. be

"Beautiful Breeze" is a gentle, soft blue. This color _will encourage_ comfort

    2. encourage

and simple designs. Designers _will use_ this color with silver or white.

    3. use

It _will_ also _go_ well with warm browns.

    4. go

"Garden Pool" is a combination of natural green and quiet blue. Next year, this cool color _will_ probably _be_ a big hit. Customers

    5. be

_will love_ this deep color. They _will enjoy_ combining it with

    6. love     7. enjoy

natural colors like beige or brown.

"Sunflower" is an energetic yellow. In the home, it _will bring_

    8. bring

a natural energy and warmth. Homeowners _will_ likely

_use_ it with calm greens and light browns.

    9. use

However you use color, next year you _will have_ a full variety of color

    10. have

choices. These color trends _will offer_ homes a fresh and modern feeling.

    11. offer

**B. Look back at the first paragraph in Activity A. Find the verbs. Complete the chart with verbs from the paragraph and the reason each verb form was used.**

|  | Example | Reason |
|---|---|---|
| 1. simple present | introduce |  |
| 2. simple past |  |  |
| 3. future with *will* |  |  |

**C. Answer the questions about your city or town and yourself. Use the future with *will*.**

1. How will your city or town be different in 50 years?

   _____

2. How will transportation be different?

   _____

3. What will stores be like?

   _____

4. In what ways will the environment be different?

   _____

5. How will you be different?

   _____

6. How will your family be different?

   _____

7. What will your job be like?

   _____

 **D. Go online for more practice with the future with *will*.**

**E. Go online for the grammar expansion.**

---

 **Unit Assignment** | **Write a proposal for a business**

 **UNIT OBJECTIVE** ▶▶▶▶

In this assignment, you will write a proposal for a new business. Your proposal will include information about what colors you will use and why. As you prepare to write, think about the Unit Question, "How do colors affect the way we feel?" Use information from Reading 1, Reading 2, the unit video, and your work in this unit to support your business proposal. Refer to the Self-Assessment checklist on page 48.

Go to the Online Writing Tutor for a writing model and alternate Unit Assignments.

# PLAN AND WRITE

**A.** **BRAINSTORM** Choose a business. Your new business could sell a product such as clothing, computers, or a type of food. Or your business could be a service such as a restaurant, repair shop, school, airline, or health service.

**B.** **PLAN** Freewrite ideas about your new business.

1. Think about these questions as you freewrite.
   - What is the name of your business?
   - What kind of business is it?
   - What colors do you want to use for your business and your advertisements?
   - Why do you want to use these colors?
   - How do you want these colors to make your customers feel?

2. Discuss your ideas with a partner. Answer any questions your partner has about your ideas. Decide which ideas are the best.

**C.** **WRITE** Use your **PLAN** notes to write your paragraph. Go to *iQ Online* to use the Online Writing Tutor.

1. Complete your new business proposal. Fill out the top part of the form. Then write a paragraph to explain your plan. Use the future with *will* when appropriate.

2. Look at the Self-Assessment checklist on page 48 to guide your writing.

---

New Business Proposal

Company name: _____

Product or service: _____

Main colors (two or three): _____

Reason for choosing these colors:

_____

_____

---

# REVISE AND EDIT

**A.** **PEER REVIEW** Read your partner's proposal. Then go online and use the Peer Review worksheet. Discuss the review with your partner.

**B.** **REWRITE** Based on your partner's review, revise and rewrite your proposal.

**C. EDIT** Complete the Self-Assessment checklist as you prepare to write the final draft of your proposal. Be prepared to hand in your work or discuss it in class.

| SELF-ASSESSMENT | | |
|---|---|---|
| Yes | No | |
| ☐ | ☐ | Do all of your ideas focus on the topic of your proposal? |
| ☐ | ☐ | Do you use the future with *will* correctly? |
| ☐ | ☐ | Do you use any adjectives with suffixes? Do you use the correct suffixes? |
| ☐ | ☐ | Does the proposal include vocabulary from this unit? |
| ☐ | ☐ | Did you check the proposal for punctuation, spelling, and grammar? |

**D. REFLECT** Go to the Online Discussion Board to discuss these questions.

1. What is something new you learned in this unit?

2. Look back at the Unit Question—How do colors affect the way we feel? Is your answer different now than when you started the unit? If yes, how is it different? Why?

# TRACK YOUR SUCCESS

**Circle the words you have learned in this unit.**

**Nouns**
advertising 🔑
bride
culture 🔑 AWL
danger 🔑
emotion 🔑
environment 🔑 AWL
feeling 🔑
psychology AWL

referee
royalty
service 🔑
variety 🔑

**Verbs**
affect 🔑 AWL
consider 🔑
encourage 🔑
establish 🔑 AWL

heal 🔑
represent 🔑

**Adjectives**
dependable
joyful
psychological AWL
specific 🔑 AWL
unaware AWL
universal 🔑

🔑 Oxford 3000™ words
AWL Academic Word List

**Check (✓) the skills you learned. If you need more work on a skill, refer to the page(s) in parentheses.**

| | |
|---|---|
| **READING** ☐ | I can get meaning from context. (p. 35) |
| **VOCABULARY** ☐ | I can use suffixes to change word forms. (p. 40) |
| **WRITING** ☐ | I can brainstorm in three different ways. (p.42) |
| **GRAMMAR** ☐ | I can use the future with *will* correctly in sentences. (p. 44) |
| **UNIT OBJECTIVE** ▶▶▶▶ ☐ | I can gather information and ideas to write a proposal that explains the colors I will use for a new business. |

| READING | ▶ | identifying supporting details |
| VOCABULARY | ▶ | prefixes |
| WRITING | ▶ | supporting your main idea with examples |
| GRAMMAR | ▶ | subject-verb agreement |

UNIT QUESTION

# What does it mean to be polite?

**A** Discuss these questions with your classmates.

1. Describe a time when someone was rude to you. What happened? What did you do?

2. Look at the photo. What is the woman doing? What do you think of her behavior?

**B** Listen to *The Q Classroom* online. Then answer these questions.

1. What examples do the students give of polite behavior?

2. Can you think of a situation when you tried to be polite but someone misunderstood you?

 **C** Go to the Online Discussion Board to discuss the Unit Question with your classmates.

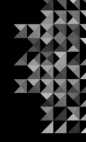

51

**D** How polite do you think you should be to these people? Check (✓) your answers. Then compare your answers with a partner.

| | A little polite | | Polite | | Very polite |
|---|---|---|---|---|---|
| | 1 | 2 | 3 | 4 | 5 |
| police officer | ☐ | ☐ | ☐ | ☐ | ☑ |
| teacher | ☐ | ☐ | ☐ | ☐ | ☐ |
| classmate | ☐ | ☐ | ☑ | ☐ | ☐ |
| brother/sister | ☐ | ☐ | ☐ | ☐ | ☐ |
| parent | ☐ | ☐ | ☐ | ☐ | ☐ |
| young child | ☐ | ☐ | ☐ | ☐ | ☐ |
| store manager | ☐ | ☐ | ☐ | ☐ | ☐ |
| sales person | ☐ | ☐ | ☐ | ☐ | ☐ |
| boss | ☐ | ☐ | ☐ | ☐ | ☐ |
| co-worker | ☐ | ☐ | ☐ | ☐ | ☐ |

**E** Think about things a parent in your culture would teach a child about being polite or rude. Write your answers in the T-chart below. Then compare your answers with a partner.

| Polite | Rude |
|---|---|
| saying "please" and "thank you" | talking loudly in public |

## READING 1 | Being Polite from Culture to Culture

You are going to read an article from a travel magazine about being polite in different cultures. Use the article to gather information and ideas for your Unit Assignment.

## PREVIEW THE READING

**A.** **VOCABULARY** Here are some words from Reading 1. Read the sentences. Then write each <u>underlined</u> word next to the correct definition.

1. I had an <u>awkward</u> conversation with my friend about money. He always borrows money and forgets to repay me.

2. Sam has really bad <u>manners</u>. He never says "please" or "thank you" to anyone, and he often talks with food in his mouth.

3. The boys dressed <u>appropriately</u> for the wedding. They wore nice suits.

4. Psychologists are interested in human <u>behavior</u>. They are studying what people do in different situations.

5. When the president entered the room, everyone stood up as a sign of <u>respect</u>.

6. Nat held his daughter's hand <u>firmly</u> when they crossed the street. He wanted to make sure she walked next to him.

7. When you have a job interview, it's important to <u>make a good impression</u>. You should dress well, arrive on time, and ask questions.

8. Laura made a <u>gesture</u> to ask the waiter to bring the check because she didn't want to shout across the restaurant.

a. _respect_ (*noun*) polite behavior toward someone or something you think is important

b. _behavior_ (*noun*) the way you act or behave

c. _awkward_ (*adjective*) not comfortable, embarrassing

*make a* d. _good impression_ (*phrasal verb*) to produce a good effect or opinion

e. _firmly_ (*adverb*) in a strong, steady way

f. _manners_ (*noun*) ways of acting that are considered polite in your society or culture *appropriate — adj*

g. **appropriately** *(adverb)* suitable or right for a particular situation

h. **gesture** *(noun)* a movement of the hand or head to express something

**iQ** ONLINE  **B.** Go online for more practice with the vocabulary.

**C.** PREVIEW  Look at the photos and the captions in the article. What do they tell you about the topic of the article?

**D.** QUICK WRITE  What are some things that might be considered polite in some cultures but not in others? Write a response before you read the article. If possible, give examples to support your answers. Be sure to use this section for your Unit Assignment.

# WORK WITH THE READING

**A.** Read the magazine article and gather information about what it means to be polite.

# Being Polite from Culture to Culture

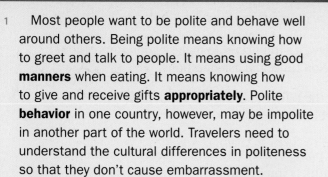

1    Most people want to be polite and behave well around others. Being polite means knowing how to greet and talk to people. It means using good **manners** when eating. It means knowing how to give and receive gifts **appropriately**. Polite **behavior** in one country, however, may be impolite in another part of the world. Travelers need to understand the cultural differences in politeness so that they don't cause embarrassment.

2    For instance, when people meet, they often shake hands. How long should a handshake be? Should you hold the other person's hand gently or **firmly**? In the United States, people prefer to shake hands firmly for a few seconds. In some Middle Eastern countries, people hold the person's hand gently for a longer time. Handshaking varies around the world.

3    What about eye contact[1]? In some countries you show **respect** when you look someone directly in the eye. In other parts of the world, to look at someone directly is rude. To be respectful, a person looks down at the ground.

4    There are also cultural differences in the way people use personal space[2]. When two people are talking, should they stand close together or far apart? Exactly how close should they stand? In North America, for instance, people usually stand about an arm's length apart during a conversation. However, in some countries in the Middle East and Latin America,

---

[1] **eye contact:** a look directly into someone else's eyes   [2] **personal space:** the area that is close to a person

In some countries making eye contact shows respect.

people stand closer. It can be **awkward** if one person likes to stand close and the other person likes to stand farther apart.

5   Three authors wrote a book *Kiss, Bow, or Shake Hands* about cultural differences. In their book, they discuss greetings, gift-giving, and time. Around the world cultures have different ideas about giving gifts. In the United States, if someone gives you a gift, you should open it while they are with you. That way they can see how happy you are to receive it. In China, you should open a gift after the person is gone.

6   Another cultural difference is time. If someone invites you to dinner at their house at 6 p.m., what time should you get there? Should you arrive early, late, or exactly on time? In Germany, it is important to arrive on time. In Argentina, polite dinner guests usually come 30 to 60 minutes after the time of the invitation. When traveling, remember that each country has a different definition of being on time.

7   A final area to be careful about is body language, including **gestures**. Is it acceptable to touch a person on the shoulder? How do you wave goodbye or hello? How do you gesture to someone to "come here"? All of these can be different from one culture to another. In Vietnam, it is rude to touch someone on the head with the palm of the hand. The gesture for "come here" in the U.S. is only used for calling animals in some other countries.

Being polite means knowing how to give and receive gifts appropriately.

8   If you are going to live, work, or study in another country, it is important to learn the language. But it is also important to learn about cultural differences. This way, you can be polite and **make a good impression**. People around you will feel comfortable and respected. Politeness and good manners can be good for making friends, good for traveling, and good for business, too.

**B.** Read the statements. Write *T* (true) or *F* (false). Then correct each false statement to make it true.

*F* 1.   Polite behavior is the same everywhere.

  is different in other cultures

*T* 2.   People make eye contact in different ways in different cultures.

_____

*F* 3.   Most people are comfortable with same amount of personal space.

_____

__F__ 4.  Being on time is important in every culture.

_is country is different_

__T__ 5.  Some gestures are polite in one country and rude in another.

_____

__F__ 6.  It's only important to know what is polite in your own country.

_Your supposed to know about other culture._

## C. Circle the answer to each question.

1.  Why do travelers need to understand cultural differences in politeness?
    a.  so they will understand the history of the country they are visiting
    b.  so no one will be embarrassed
    c.  so they will feel better about themselves

2.  How do people in the United States prefer to shake hands?
    a.  firmly for a short time
    b.  gently for a short time
    c.  firmly for a long time

3.  How closely do people in Latin America or the Middle East like to stand while talking?
    a.  at an arm's length
    b.  more than an arm's length
    c.  more closely than an arm's length

4.  What should you do if someone in China gives you a gift?
    a.  open it in front of the person
    b.  wait until the person has left before opening it
    c.  open the gift immediately

5.  You are invited for dinner at 7:00 p.m. in Germany. What time should you arrive?
    a.  6:30 p.m.          b.  7:00 p.m.          c.  7:30 p.m.

6.  If you show that you understand cultural differences and politeness, how will people feel?
    a.  comfortable and respected
    b.  uncomfortable and awkward
    c.  polite and happy

**D.** Complete the chart. Use countries or regions and topics from the boxes.

| Countries / Regions | | Topics | |
|---|---|---|---|
| Argentina | Latin America | gestures | personal space |
| China | Middle Eastern countries | gift-giving | time |
| Germany | North America | greetings | |
| United States | | | |
| Vietnam | | | |

| Paragraph Number | Country or Region | Topic |
|---|---|---|
| 2 | United States, Middle Eastern countries | greetings |
| 4 | North America Middle East Latin America | Personal space |
| 5 | U.S China | gift |
| 6 | Germany Argentina | Time |
| 7 | Vietnam U.S | gestures |

**Critical Thinking** Tip

Activity E asks you to **discuss** your ideas. **Discussing** your ideas with other people helps you to consider ideas you might not have thought about on your own.

**E. Discuss these questions in a group.**

1. What are some examples of what it means to be polite?

2. In what ways is shaking hands different in different parts of the world?

3. What is the comfortable distance for conversation in North America? Is it the same where you live?

4. If you are invited to lunch in Germany at 12:00, what time should you arrive? Is it the same where you live?

5. How does being polite help you make a good impression?

 **F.** Go online to read *Politeness in American Culture* and check your comprehension.

 **WRITE WHAT YOU THINK**

**A. Ask and answer the questions with a partner.**

1. How do people use personal space differently in different parts of the world?

2. Why do you think body language is different from one culture to another?

**B.** Choose one of the questions in Activity A on page 57 and write a response. Use supporting examples. Look back at your Quick Write on page 54 as you think about what you learned.

---

**Reading Skill** | **Identifying supporting details**

A well-written article includes **details** that support the main ideas. Details can be facts, reasons, or examples. Identifying supporting details will help you understand the main ideas of an article.

Main Idea — Bowing is a form of greeting in many countries.

Supporting Details

**fact:** something you know is true — Bowing is the traditional greeting in East Asia.

**reason:** the cause of something — People bow low when greeting older people because it is a sign of respect.

**example:** something that shows what something is like — In a very formal bow, the forehead sometimes touches the floor.

Identifying and underlining important supporting details as you read can help you improve your reading comprehension.

---

**A.** Reread paragraph 4 in Reading 1. Look at the main idea of the paragraph. Write two details that support it. Then compare your answers with a partner.

_____

_____

**B.** Reread paragraph 5. Answer the questions. Then compare your answers with a partner.

1. What is the main idea? _____

2. How many supporting details are in the paragraph? What are they?

_____

_____

**C.** Reread paragraph 6. Answer the questions. Then compare your answers with a partner.

1. What is the main idea? _____

2. What examples does the writer use as supporting details?

   _____

   _____

 **D.** Go online for more practice with identifying supporting details.

# READING 2 | Answers to All Your Travel Questions

 You are going to read an online discussion board with questions and advice about customs in different countries. Use the posts to gather information and ideas for your Unit Assignment.

## PREVIEW THE READING

**Vocabulary Skill Review**

In Unit 2, you learned about using suffixes to expand vocabulary. Add the suffixes –ful or –al to the following nouns to change them to adjectives: *respect, culture, tradition.* Use your dictionary to check spelling.

**A.** **VOCABULARY** Here are some words from Reading 2. Read the sentences. Circle the answer that best matches the meaning of each underlined word or phrase.

1. My uncle gave me some good <u>advice</u> about starting a business.
   a. money that someone loans you
   b. proverbs or famous quotes
   c. words that help someone decide what to do

2. A <u>custom</u> you will notice when you go to Japan is that people don't wear their shoes inside their homes.
   a. way of life          b. thing for sale          c. idea

3. It's rude to <u>interrupt</u> someone when they are speaking. You should always let them finish.
   a. make someone stop talking
   b. repeat something over and over
   c. whisper; talk quietly

4. I want to <u>take part in</u> the meeting about the neighborhood school. I think it's going to be very interesting.
   a. divide up; separate
   b. join, participate in
   c. act in

5. Classes at many universities are <u>informal</u>. Students can bring food to class and ask questions whenever they want. Adj
   a. lengthy; taking a long time
   b. relaxed and friendly
   c. useful and informative

6. It's <u>traditional</u> in some countries for the bride to wear a white dress for the wedding. In other countries the bride wears red.
   a. inexpensive
   b. doing what others want you to do
   c. ways of doing things that have existed for a long time

7. Try to <u>avoid</u> talking when you have food in your mouth. It's very rude!
   a. choose not to do        b. adjust        c. continue

8. On a <u>typical</u> day, Erik works from 9:00 a.m. to 5:00 p.m., but today he worked until 7:30 p.m.
   a. pleasant        b. awkward        c. usual

**B.** Go online for more practice with the vocabulary.

**C.** **PREVIEW** In this online discussion board, travelers ask for advice about customs in different countries. What kinds of topics do you think the travelers will ask about?
- ☑ greeting people          ☐ giving/receiving gifts
- ☐ conversation topics      ☑ table manners
- ☐ other _____

**D.** **QUICK WRITE** Choose one of the topics in Activity C. What are some of the customs in your country? What about in other countries? Write a few sentences. Be sure to use this section for your Unit Assignment.

# WORK WITH THE READING

**A.** Read the posts from the online discussion board and gather information about what it means to be polite.

## Answers to All Your Travel Questions

| | |
|---|---|
| Yong Jun Park, Seoul<br>Posted:<br>3 days ago | **Question:** First trip to U.S.<br>For my new job, I will travel to the United States next month and meet my American boss. This will be my first trip to the U.S. I'm worried about correct business etiquette[1] and manners. My boss invited me to his home for dinner. Do you have any **advice**? |
| Sue, Miami<br>Posted:<br>3 days ago | **1. Re:** First trip to U.S.<br>It's a good idea to bring a small gift or something from your country. Don't be surprised if your boss opens the gift right away. In the U.S., people often open a gift when they receive it. In Korea, that is not polite, but it's appropriate in the U.S. |
| Jun, Seoul<br>Posted:<br>2 days ago | **2. Re:** First trip to U.S.<br>Many Americans are very **informal** at home. One time I went to dinner at the home of an American business partner. I was surprised that everyone stood and talked in the kitchen while the husband and wife cooked dinner. Also, unlike in Korea, everyone **took part in** the dinner table conversation, even the man's wife and children. |
| Andrea, Santiago<br>Posted:<br>12 hours ago | **3. Re:** First trip to U.S.<br>I agree with Jun. I was surprised that American men often cook and that both the husband and wife come to the dinner table and talk. You probably won't speak about business during dinner, so my advice is to know some good topics of conversation. For example, you can talk about travel, food, or sports. Of course, it's good to ask about your boss's family. But it's not polite to ask questions about age, salary, religion, or politics. |
| Sun Hee Choi, Pusan<br>Posted:<br>8 hours ago | **4. Re:** First trip to U.S.<br>Americans use their hands to eat some kinds of food, such as pizza and fried chicken. Watch your American hosts[2], and do what they do. |
| Kathryn, New York<br>Posted:<br>5 hours ago | **5. Re:** First trip to U.S.<br>In Korea and Japan, it's the **custom** to remove your shoes before entering a house. In the United States, you usually don't take your shoes off. Once I was traveling in Japan and entered a house with my shoes on by mistake. Oops! |

---

[1] **etiquette:** polite and correct behavior in a social situation      [2] **hosts:** people who have visitors to the home and entertain them

| | |
|---|---|
| Yong Jun Park, Seoul<br>Posted:<br>2 hours ago | **6. Re:** First trip to U.S.<br>It sounds like Americans are so informal. I'll try to be informal and polite.<br>I hope I do the right thing. Thanks for all the advice! One more question:<br>What's an appropriate gift for me to bring my boss and his family? |
| Sam, Los Angeles<br>Posted:<br>4 days ago | **Question:** Travel to Egypt<br>Any tips on table manners in Egypt? I'll be there on business, and I'm sure we will have business dinners. Also, anything else that's important to know? |
| Khalid, Cairo<br>Posted:<br>12 hours ago | **1. Re:** Travel to Egypt<br>Egypt is a **traditional** country, and it has many customs that are different from the U.S. Table manners are similar to the U.S., but there are a few important differences. For instance, it's impolite to use your left hand to eat. Be sure to read about Egyptian culture before you go. You can **avoid** embarrassing yourself. |
| Carlos, Madrid<br>Posted:<br>2 hours ago | **2. Re:** Travel to Egypt<br>I traveled to Egypt on business last year and saw two interesting differences in business. First, unlike Americans, Egyptians don't discuss business at the beginning of business meetings. Instead they begin with informal conversation. This is because personal relationships are very important in Egyptian business. Second, during a meeting in Egypt, it's common for others to come in the room and **interrupt** the meeting. In the United States, it's rude to interrupt a meeting. In Egypt, these interruptions are **typical**! |

**B. Read the statements. Write _T_ (true) or _F_ (false). Then correct each false statement to make it true.**

_F_ 1.  Yong Jun Park is worried about his English.

_____

_T_ 2.  It is appropriate to bring a small gift when visiting a home in the U.S.

_____

_F_ 3.  Many Americans are very formal at home.

_____

_T_ 4.  It's a good idea to know several different topics of conversation.

_____

_F_ 5.  Carlos thinks business customs are the same in Egypt and in the U.S.

_____DIFFERENT._____

**C.** Write information from the online discussion board for each of the topics below.

1. when to open gifts
   a. in South Korea ___theater, not polite.___
   b. in the U.S. ___right away___

2. conversation topics in the U.S.
   a. good topics ___travel, food and sports___
   b. impolite topics ___about age, salary, religion or politics.___

3. wearing shoes in the house
   a. in Japan and South Korea ___remove before entering.___
   b. in the U.S. ___you usually don't take your shoes off___

4. beginning business meetings
   a. in the U.S. ___discuss business___
   b. in Egypt ___informal conversation the beginning of the meeting.___

5. interruptions in business meetings
   a. in Egypt ___these interruptions are typical!___
   b. in the U.S. ___it's rude to interrupt a meeting.___

**D.** Complete the sentences with words from the box.

| conversation | informal | kitchen | manners | relationships |
| hosts | interrupt | left | polite | shoes |

Some people who travel are worried about etiquette

and ___manners___ because customs may be different
       1

from one country to another. For example, many Americans are

___informal___ at home. It isn't unusual for conversations
     2

to take place in the ___kitchen___ while preparing a
                        3

meal. Travel, food, or sports are ___polite___ topics for
                                     4

conversation. If you aren't sure what to do when eating, you can watch

your ___hosts___.
        5

In the U.S., it isn't necessary to remove your ___shoes___
when entering a house. If you travel to Egypt, you should be careful not to

eat with your ___left___ hand. At business meetings in

Egypt, it is common to begin with informal ___conversation___
because personal ___relationships___ are important in

Egyptian business. You should also expect to have people come in and

___interrupt___ while the meeting is taking place.

**E.** **Discuss these questions with a partner or in a group.**

1. What are some examples of good table manners?

2. If guests from another country visit you, should they adapt to the behavior
in your culture, or should you try to make them feel at home by doing
things their way?

## WRITE WHAT YOU THINK

**A.** **Discuss the questions in a group. Look back at your Quick Write on page 60 as you think about what you learned.**

1. Why is it important for a businessperson to understand another culture
when traveling?

2. Sun Hee writes, "Watch your American host and do what they do." Is this
good advice? Why or why not?

**B.** **Go online to watch the video about using cell phones in public places. Then check your comprehension.**

**C.** Think about the unit video, Reading 1, and Reading 2 as you discuss these questions. Then choose one question and write a response.

1. Do you think that people today are less polite than in the past? Why?

2. Do you think that people are naturally polite? Or do they learn to be polite? Explain.

## Vocabulary Skill    Prefixes

**Tip for Success**

Not every word starting with *in-*, *im-*, or *un-* has a prefix meaning *not*. For example, these words do not have negative prefixes: *interrupt*, *impression*, *uncle*.

A **prefix** is a group of letters at the beginning of a word. Adding a prefix to a word changes its meaning. Understanding prefixes will help you increase your vocabulary. The prefixes *in-*, *im-*, and *un-* mean *not* and are added to adjectives.

There are no rules for when to use *in-* or *un-*. You need to learn these words or use a dictionary to help you.

| | | | |
|---|---|---|---|
| **in**formal | not formal | **un**able | not able |
| **in**visible | not visible | **un**usual | not usual |

*Im-* is added to an adjective that starts with *m* or *p*.

| | |
|---|---|
| **im**mature | not mature |
| **im**polite | not polite |

**A.** Look at the words below. Add the correct prefix to each word. Then write the new words in the chart. Check your answers in a dictionary.

| | | | |
|---|---|---|---|
| ~~appropriate~~ | common | formal | possible |
| clear | dependable | perfect | traditional |
| comfortable | expensive | polite | usual |

| in- | im- | un- |
|---|---|---|
| inappropriate | Imperfect | Unusual |
| Informal | Impossible | Uncomfortable |
| Inexpensive | Impolite | Uncommon |
| Insufficient | Impersonal | Unclear |
| Incorrect | | Untraditional |
| Inexperienced | | Undependable |
| Incredible | | Unbelievable |
| Incompetent | | |

**B. Complete the sentences with words from Activity A on page 65. Use the word with or without the prefix. For some sentences, there is more than one correct answer.**

1. My brother is very _dependable_. He always does what he says he will do.

2. The directions were confusing and _unclear_. Kenan got lost three times trying to get to the restaurant.

3. Because her first name was so _uncommon_, _unusual_, she always had to repeat it several times.

4. It's _impossible_ for me to finish the project on time. I have too much research to do. I can't do it.

5. Our receptionist is very friendly and welcoming. She makes people feel _comfortable_ when they come into the office.

6. Although it was a small and _inexpensive_ gift, it was very thoughtful. The cost wasn't important.

7. The customer was very _impolite_. He was so rude that no one wanted to help him.

8. Many people send quick email invitations to celebrations, but Jamal sent a _traditional_ _formal_ invitation in the mail to his graduation. He chose very expensive paper.

9. The bed was very _uncomfortable_ so I barely slept all night and I had a backache in the morning.

10. In the U.S. it's _inappropriate_ to ask how old people are or how much money they make.

iQ ONLINE **C. Go online for more practice with prefixes.**

# WRITING

 At the end of this unit, you will write a paragraph in response to a question from an online discussion board. This paragraph will include specific examples from the readings and your own ideas.

## Writing Skill    Supporting your main idea with examples

When you write a paragraph, support your main idea with **examples**. Examples will make your ideas clear to your readers.

Writers often introduce examples with the phrases *for example* and *for instance*.

> My advice is to know good topics of conversation. For example, you can talk about travel, food, or sports.

**A.** **WRITING MODEL** Read this model response to Yong Jun Park's question from Reading 2, *What's an appropriate gift for me to bring my boss and his family?* Circle the main idea of the response. Underline the examples. Then highlight any words that the writer uses to introduce examples.

It's difficult to select the right gift to bring a host, especially if you don't know the person or the culture very well. However, there are several appropriate gifts to bring a host. For example, you can bring flowers. Buy a nice bouquet of flowers from a florist or even at the supermarket. Be sure to take the price tag off, though. Food is another good example of an appropriate item to bring. Ask the host what you can bring, or bring something everybody will probably enjoy, like a basket of fruit. If you don't want to bring food or flowers, be creative. For instance, you can bring a small gift for the home. Think of something that people use even if they already have it. Soap and hand towels are a good idea.

**B.** Complete the sentences. Use information from Reading 1 and Reading 2.

1. The idea of personal space is different from one country to another. For example,

   _____

2. In the United States, you should shake hands firmly. This is not true everywhere, however. For instance, _____

3. In Latin America, people don't always arrive exactly on time. For instance,

_____

4. In many Asian countries it is rude to open a gift right away. However, in some countries you should open a gift immediately. For example,

_____

5. The idea of politeness can vary from one country to another. For instance,

_____

**C.** Read the main idea and supporting detail in the chart below. Then add more supporting ideas.

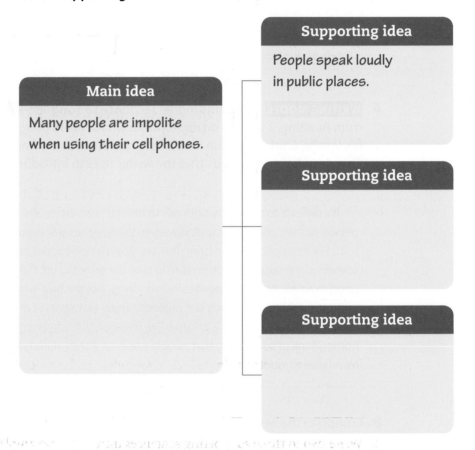

**Main idea**

Many people are impolite when using their cell phones.

**Supporting idea**

People speak loudly in public places.

**Supporting idea**

**Supporting idea**

**D.** Copy the topic and concluding sentences below. Then complete the paragraph. Give examples to support the main idea in the topic sentence. Use the information from the chart in Activity C.

**Topic sentence:** Many people do not have good cell phone manners, and they are impolite when they use their phones. For example, …

**Concluding sentence:** …If cell phone users were more thoughtful of others, they might be more polite.

**E.** Choose one of the topics below. Then use the chart to show your main idea and two or three examples giving short answers.

Topic A: Do you think it is important for children to show respect for their parents? What are some ways they can do this?

Topic B: Should you study the customs of another country before you visit? What are some things you should learn before traveling to another country?

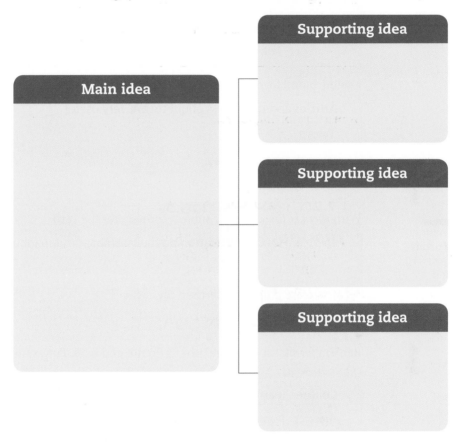

**F.** Write a complete paragraph giving examples. Use your notes from Activity E.

1. Write a topic sentence introducing your idea. Make it clear which topic you chose in Activity E.

_____

2. Write two to three supporting sentences introducing examples.

_____

_____

_____

 **G.** Go online for more practice with supporting your main idea with examples.

It is important to make sure that the subject and verb in a sentence agree. Use the singular form of the verb with singular subjects.

My **aunt** always **speaks** in a very loud voice.
subject       verb

The **cake is** delicious.
subject verb

Use the plural form of the verb with plural subjects.

**Articles** about business etiquette **are** very useful.
subject                                verb

My **cats eat** twice a day.
subject  verb

With *there is/there are*, the subject comes after the verb.

There **is** a lot of **information** on the Internet about manners.
verb          subject

There **are** fifteen **students** in my class.
verb          subject

Remember that some plural nouns do not end in -*s*. For example, *people*, *children*, *police*.

**Children learn** manners from their parents.
subject    verb

**A. Circle the subject in each sentence. Then complete the sentence with the correct form of the verb. The first one has been done for you.**

1. My (brother) _____lives_____ (live) in Boston.

2. There _____IS_____ (be) a (man) waiting outside for Paulo.

3. The police in my neighborhood _____are_____ (be) very helpful.

4. People _____uses_____ (use) the Internet to get all kinds of information.

5. This book _____gives_____ (give) helpful advice on business travel.

**B.** Read this post from a Web page. Circle the subject and underline the verb in each sentence. Then correct the errors in subject-verb agreement.

> In my opinion, the most annoying habit is talking on cell phones. People
> ~~is~~ *are* talking on their cell phones all the time. My brother always interrupt our
> conversations and answers his phone. People like my brother ~~doesn't~~ *don't* care about
> manners. People talk on cell phones in restaurants and in doctors' offices. There
> ~~is~~ *are* times when cell phones are very annoying. Cell phones ring and interrupts our
> thoughts. People need to show more respect for others. There is appropriate and
> *are*
> inappropriate places to use cell phones.

**C.** Look back at your paragraph in Activity F on page 69. Check subject-verb agreement. Circle the subject and underline the verb in each sentence.

**D.** Go online for more practice with subject-verb agreement.

**E.** Go online for the grammar expansion.

---

**Unit Assignment**   Write a paragraph with supporting examples

---

**UNIT OBJECTIVE** ▶▶▶▶   In this assignment, you will write a paragraph in response to a question posted on an online discussion board about politeness. As you prepare your paragraph, think about the Unit Question, "What does it mean to be polite?" Use information from Reading 1, Reading 2, the unit video, and your work in this unit to support your paragraph. Refer to the Self-Assessment checklist on page 72.

   Go to the Online Writing Tutor for a writing model and alternate Unit Assignments.

## PLAN AND WRITE

**Critical Thinking** Tip

When you are writing an opinion, try to also think about the opposite point of view. How can you make your ideas stronger?

**A.** **BRAINSTORM** Read the following questions from an online discussion board. Choose which question you want to answer for your paragraph. Then freewrite your ideas about the question.

1.  I'm traveling to the United States for the first time. What do you know about manners in the U.S.? What tips do you have about being polite?

2.  I think that people today are very rude. I'm the father of two young boys, ages five and ten. How can I teach my sons to be polite?

**B.** **PLAN** Complete these activities.

1. Write a topic sentence for your paragraph. Your topic sentence should answer the question you chose and contain your controlling idea.

2. Write as many examples as you can. Use your ideas from Activity A to help you.

3. Discuss your topic sentence and examples with a partner. Circle the examples that best support your topic sentence.

 **C.** **WRITE** Use your **PLAN** notes to write your paragraph. Go to *iQ Online* to use the Online Writing Tutor.

1. As you write, be sure that your examples support your main idea.

2. Look at the Self-Assessment checklist to guide your writing.

## REVISE AND EDIT

 **A.** **PEER REVIEW** Read your partner's paragraph. Then go online and use the Peer Review worksheet. Discuss the review with your partner.

**B.** **REWRITE** Based on your partner's review, revise and rewrite your paragraph.

**C.** **EDIT** Complete the Self-Assessment checklist as you prepare to write the final draft of your paragraph. Be prepared to hand in your work or discuss it in class.

| SELF-ASSESSMENT | | |
|---|---|---|
| Yes | No | |
| ☐ | ☐ | Do all your examples support your main idea? |
| ☐ | ☐ | Do the subjects and verbs agree? |
| ☐ | ☐ | Do you use adjectives with prefixes correctly? |
| ☐ | ☐ | Does your paragraph include vocabulary from this unit? |
| ☐ | ☐ | Did you check the paragraph for punctuation, spelling, and grammar? |

 **D.** **REFLECT** Go to the Online Discussion Board to discuss these questions.

1. What is something new you learned in this unit?

2. Look back at the Unit Question—What does it mean to be polite? Is your answer different now than when you started the unit? If yes, how is it different? Why?

# TRACK YOUR SUCCESS

**Circle the words and phrases you have learned in this unit.**

**Nouns**
advice 🔑
behavior 🔑
custom 🔑
gesture
manners
respect 🔑

**Verbs**
avoid 🔑
interrupt 🔑

**Adjectives**
awkward 🔑
informal 🔑
traditional 🔑 AWL
typical 🔑

**Adverbs**
appropriately AWL
firmly 🔑

**Phrases**
make a good impression
take part in

🔑 Oxford 3000™ words
AWL Academic Word List

**Check (✓) the skills you learned. If you need more work on a skill, refer to the page(s) in parentheses.**

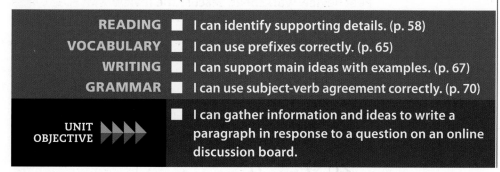

| | |
|---|---|
| **READING** ■ | I can identify supporting details. (p. 58) |
| **VOCABULARY** ■ | I can use prefixes correctly. (p. 65) |
| **WRITING** ■ | I can support main ideas with examples. (p. 67) |
| **GRAMMAR** ■ | I can use subject-verb agreement correctly. (p. 70) |
| **UNIT OBJECTIVE** ▶▶▶ ■ | I can gather information and ideas to write a paragraph in response to a question on an online discussion board. |

READING ▶ taking notes
VOCABULARY ▶ using the dictionary
WRITING ▶ writing an opinion paragraph
GRAMMAR ▶ modals

UNIT QUESTION

# What makes a competition unfair?

**A** Discuss these questions with your classmates.

1. What sports do you like to play? What sports do you like to watch?

2. Look at the photo. What are these people doing?

**B** Listen to *The Q Classroom* online. Then answer these questions.

1. Do you think that the home team has an advantage? Why or why not?

2. Can you give an example of cheating in sports?

 **C** Go to the Online Discussion Board to discuss the Unit Question with your classmates.

**D** Circle the answer that makes each statement true for you.

a. I (*often* / *sometimes* / *rarely*) watch sports on TV.

b. I think professional athletes' salaries are (*too high* / *about right* / *too low*).

c. I think most Olympic competitions are (*fair* / *unfair*).

**E** Look at the list of sports below. Which sports do you think are the most interesting to watch? Write the sports in order from *most interesting (1)* to *least interesting (8)*. Then discuss your answers with a partner.

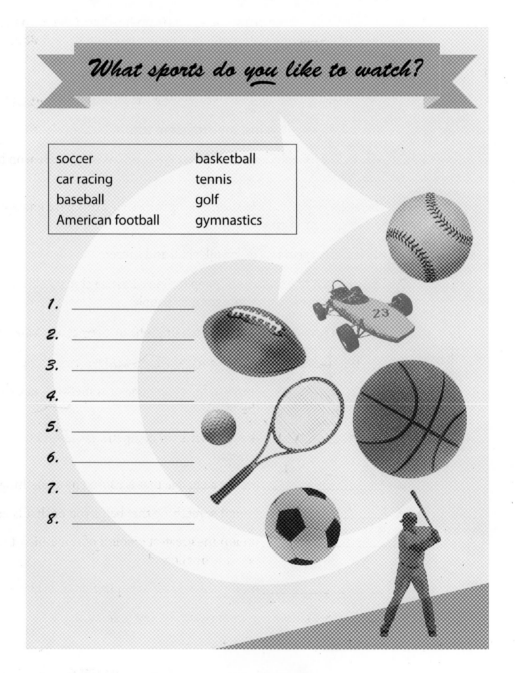

*What sports do you like to watch?*

| | |
|---|---|
| soccer | basketball |
| car racing | tennis |
| baseball | golf |
| American football | gymnastics |

1. _____

2. _____

3. _____

4. _____

5. _____

6. _____

7. _____

8. _____

## READING 1 | Money and Sports

 You are going to read an article about money and professional soccer teams. Use the article to gather information and ideas for your Unit Assignment.

### PREVIEW THE READING

**A.** **VOCABULARY** Here are some words from Reading 1. Read the sentences. Then write each <u>underlined</u> word next to the correct definition.

1. Ramón is tall for his age, so he has an <u>advantage</u> when he plays basketball.
   *Noun*

2. Our baseball team was very strong. We won the state <u>championship</u>.
   *Noun*

3. When I <u>compete</u> against my brother in tennis, I usually lose.

4. Andy's new bike had an immediate <u>effect</u> on his results. He won his next three races.

5. The team's <u>financial</u> situation is very bad. They don't have enough money to buy new uniforms.

6. My favorite sports <u>include</u> volleyball and soccer.

7. The <u>limit</u> for the number of people allowed in the club's swimming pool is 45. It is unsafe with more than 45 people.

8. Our soccer coach had a <u>solution</u> to our problem. She had us change positions.

a. _compete_ (*verb*) to try to win or achieve something

b. _include_ (*verb*) to have someone or something as a part of the whole

c. _championship_ (*noun*) a series of competitions to find the best player or team

d. _effect_ (*noun*) a change that is caused by something; a result

e. _advantage_ (*noun*) something that helps you or that is useful

f. _limit_ (*noun*) the greatest amount of something that is possible or allowed

g. _solution_ (*noun*) the answer to a question or problem

h. _Financial_ (*adjective*) connected with money

**C.** PREVIEW  Scan the article to find the names of three teams and two people. To find the answers quickly, scan for capital letters. Then look at the title of the article. What do you think these teams and players have in common?

**D.** QUICK WRITE  Do you think wealthy teams are usually better teams? Why or why not? Write a short paragraph to answer the question. If possible, give examples to support your opinion. Be sure to use this section for your Unit Assignment.

## WORK WITH THE READING

**A.** Read the magazine article and gather information about what makes a competition unfair.

# Money and Sports

1    "Goal!" shouts the announcer. It is a familiar sound for Real Madrid these days. They have just scored another goal against a visiting team. Compared to Madrid, the other side looks weak. The visiting players know that it is almost impossible to win a game against such a strong team. Real Madrid has better players, better coaches, better equipment, and better salaries. They have something that many teams don't have: a lot of money. This gives their club an unfair **advantage** over other teams that are not as wealthy.

2    Real Madrid is now the richest soccer team in the world, with England's Manchester United the second richest. Madrid is worth more than $3.3 billion. Manchester United is worth more than $3.1 billion and Barcelona is worth $2.6 billion. These clubs have enough money to pay the high salaries of the best players in the world.

For example, Cristiano Ronaldo used to play for Manchester United. Now he is Madrid's top player and earns $21.9 million per year. The richest clubs can pay the highest salaries of the best players. Other wealthy clubs **include** Arsenal, Bayern Munich, and AC Milan. As a result, these clubs have been very successful. For example, Real Madrid has won nine European Cup **championships**, more than any other team. Between 2003 and 2013, all but two of the European Cup champions were from the 10 wealthiest teams. Money is a clear advantage for these soccer teams.

3    The wealthiest teams make money in several ways. First, they can sell tickets at high prices because fans[1] want to see the top players in action. Second, television stations pay the teams to broadcast their games. Third, large companies give **financial** support to the best teams. These corporate sponsors[2] pay

---

[1] **fans:** people who are very enthusiastic about something
[2] **corporate sponsors:** companies that help pay for special sports events

money so that their company name can be on the clubs' shirts, shoes, and stadiums.

4    The recent success of the English team Chelsea shows an example of the **effect** of money on a team. For many years, Chelsea was a club with little money and few wins. They didn't have a lot of money to pay good players. Their last championship win was in 1955. Everything changed in 2003 when Russian billionaire Roman Abramovich bought the team for $233 million. In his first year, Abramovich spent more than $350 million on players. By 2006, Chelsea had won two championships. Now Chelsea is one of the richest clubs in the world.

5    Many sports fans feel that money in sports creates an unfair advantage. Some teams have so much money that it seems impossible for poorer clubs to beat them. Wealthy teams are usually more successful, so they sell more tickets and make more money. Teams that do not have as much money usually are not as successful. It is difficult for them to get money from tickets, television, and corporate sponsors. Sports fans know that money gives some clubs a great advantage.

6    There are no easy **solutions** to this problem, but there are some possibilities. Some people think that rich teams could share some of

Sports fans love close competition between athletes.

their money with the poorer ones. This way, the poorer teams would be able to pay higher salaries for better players. Another solution is to put a **limit** on the amount of money that teams can spend on players' salaries. This way, the players' salaries would not continue to rise so much. However, finding and agreeing upon the best solution is very complicated.

7    Sports fans love close competitions between athletes, but everyone wants teams to **compete** fairly. Fair competitions do not seem possible when there are a small number of teams that are very wealthy. Money creates unfair advantages in professional sports, and although there are no easy answers, we should continue to search for ways to make sports fair.

| World's Richest Soccer Clubs in 2013 | | | | |
|---|---|---|---|---|
| Rank | Team | Country | Value ($mil) | Yearly Revenue ($mil) |
| 1 | Real Madrid | Spain | 3,300 | 650 |
| 2 | Manchester United | England | 3,265 | 502 |
| 3 | Barcelona | Spain | 2,600 | 613 |
| 4 | Arsenal | England | 1,326 | 368 |
| 5 | Bayern Munich | Germany | 1,309 | 468 |
| 6 | AC Milan | Italy | 945 | 326 |
| 7 | Chelsea | England | 901 | 409 |
| 8 | Juventus | Italy | 694 | 248 |
| 9 | Manchester City | England | 689 | 362 |
| 10 | Liverpool | England | 651 | 296 |

Note: *Value* is how much the club is worth. *Yearly Revenue* is how much the club makes every year from ticket sales, TV time, and so on.

**Sources:** "Soccer Team Values," *Forbes* Magazine, May 7, 2014; "Money and Sports," from "Soccer Team Valuations," *Forbes* Magazine, April 8, 2009; "Soccer's Richest Clubs Get Richer," by Jack Gage; "In Pictures: 20 Top-Earning Players," by Paul Maidment and Christina Settimi and "The World's Best Paid Soccer Players," by Christina Settimi from *Forbes* Magazine, April 30, 2008.

**B. Read the statements. Write _T_ (true) or _F_ (false). Then correct each false statement to make it true.**

_____ 1. The wealthiest teams can attract the best players.

_____

_T_ 2. The wealthiest teams are usually the most successful.

_____

_F_ 3. The wealthiest teams sell their tickets at low prices.

_____

_T_ 4. Many sports fans feel that wealthy teams have an unfair advantage.

_____

_F_ 5. There are some easy solutions to the problem of wealthy teams having an unfair advantage.

_____

**C. Answer these questions.**

1. According to the article, which soccer team is the richest in the world?

_____

2. How much money did Cristiano Ronaldo earn at the time this article was written? Do you think he earned more when he played for Manchester United or when he played for Real Madrid?

   21.9 million

3. What do corporate sponsors do for a team?

   Financial support

4. In the article, what are the two suggested solutions to the problem of money in sports?

   Limit

5. How are wealthy teams able to make money? Explain the three ways.

   Take prices,

6. What happened in 2003 that changed the success of the Chelsea team?

_____

**D. Complete the sentences. Use information from the chart on page 79.**

1. England has _____ 5 _____ of the wealthiest teams, while Spain has _____ 2 _____ .

2. The value of Bayern Munich is just a little less than _____ Arsenal .

3. Overall, the higher the rank, the higher the _____ .

4. The team with the highest yearly revenue is _____ real madrid

5. The team with the lowest yearly revenue has a rank of _____ 8 _____ .

**E. Discuss with a partner the two suggested solutions in the article. Think of a third solution and add it to the chart. Fill in the chart with the advantages and disadvantages of each solution. Then complete the sentences, giving your opinion of the best solution.**

| Money and professional soccer teams | | |
|---|---|---|
| **Solutions** | **Advantages** | **Disadvantages** |
| **1.** | | |
| **2.** | | |
| **3.** | | |

In my opinion, the best solution is to _____

because _____ .

Although _____

_____ .

**iQ ONLINE** **F. Go online to read *An Unusual Game* and check your comprehension.**

# WRITE WHAT YOU THINK

**A.** Ask and answer the questions with a partner.

1. What other sports have wealthy teams and poor teams? Do they have the same problems described in Reading 1?

2. Professional athletes earn very high salaries. Do you think their salaries are too high? Why or why not?

**B.** Choose one of the questions in Activity A and write a response. Look back at your Quick Write on page 78 as you think about what you learned.

## Reading Skill   Taking notes

When you read an article or textbook, it is helpful to **take notes** while you read. You can write notes directly in the book next to the text. Taking notes can help you remember what you read. When you take notes, you do not need to write complete sentences. You can write short phrases or even just a few words. You can also underline or highlight important information.

Some things you might note are:

- main ideas
- supporting ideas
- important names, dates, or numbers

You can use your notes for summarizing, answering questions, comparing ideas, or studying for a test.

**A.** Take notes on Reading 1.

1. Reread paragraph 3 in Reading 1 on pages 78 and 79. Make notes in the margin beside the main idea and three supporting ideas.

2. Reread paragraph 4 in Reading 1 on page 79. Highlight the important names and numbers.

3. Reread paragraph 6 in Reading 1 on page 79. Underline the main idea and two supporting ideas.

**B.** Work with a partner. Compare your notes from Activity A.

 **C.** Go online for more practice with taking notes.

# READING 2 | The Technology Advantage

 **UNIT OBJECTIVE** You are going to read an online article about technology in sports. Use the article to gather information and ideas for your Unit Assignment.

## PREVIEW THE READING

**Vocabulary Skill Review**

In Unit 3, you learned about using prefixes to expand vocabulary. Add the prefixes *in-*, *im-*, or *un-* to the following words from Readings 1 and 2: *complicated, expensive, possible, safe, successful.* Use your dictionary to check spelling.

**A. VOCABULARY** Here are some words from Reading 2. Read their definitions. Then complete each sentence.

> **artificial** (*adjective*) 🔑 made or produced to copy something natural; not real
> **ban** (*verb*) 🔑 to officially say that something is not allowed
> **energy** (*noun*) 🔑 strength and ability to be active without getting tired
> **equipment** (*noun*) 🔑 the things that are needed to do a particular activity
> **invent** (*verb*) 🔑 to think of or make something for the first time
> **performance** (*noun*) 🔑 how well or badly you do something; how well or badly something works
> **reason** (*noun*) 🔑 the cause of something; something that explains why something happens
> **technology** (*noun*) 🔑 the scientific knowledge or equipment that is needed for a particular industry

🔑 Oxford 3000™ words

1. Airline companies agreed to _____ban_____ smoking on airplanes many years ago. Now smoking is not allowed on any flights.

2. Playing sports requires a lot of _____energy_____, so athletes need to eat healthy foods and drink plenty of water.

3. Many professional sports stadiums have ___artificial___ grass, which requires less care and attention than real grass.

4. The ___reason___ for my low test score became clear: I had studied the wrong unit.

5. After hiring a new coach, the ice skater's ___performance___ greatly improved. Her scores in competitions were much higher.

6. Running is a popular sport because it is great exercise, and it doesn't require a lot of special ___equipment___. All you need are running shoes.

7. My friend is a very creative cook. He likes to _____invent_____ new recipes for unusual dishes.

8. New _____technology_____ is helping improve sports equipment. Now athletes can ski, bike, and swim even faster.

iQ ONLINE **B.** Go online for more practice with the vocabulary.

**C.** PREVIEW Preview the reading. Read the first paragraph, the first sentence of each supporting paragraph, and the last paragraph. What would be the best subtitle for the article? Check (✓) your answer.

☐ The Technology Advantage: Computer Companies Support Sports Teams

☐ The Technology Advantage: Improve Your Video Game Skills

☑ The Technology Advantage: Better Equipment, Better Performance

**D.** QUICK WRITE What are some examples of how technology is improving equipment for athletes? Think, for example, of how technology may improve skis, tennis racquets, or running shoes. Write a few sentences about the topic. Be sure to use this section for your Unit Assignment.

New technology is helping athletes. From high-tech clothing to artificial arm and legs. Example, a years ago sports engineers. Invented a new material for swimsuits. It like as shark skin. Most importantly, the material sends more oxigen to swimm muscles. and make then swim faster and float better.

# WORK WITH THE READING

**A.** Read the article and gather information about what makes a competition unfair.

# The Technology Advantage

1   Since ancient times, athletes have always looked for ways to win competitions. Athletes can be winners with better training, better coaching, and better food. They can also improve **performance** with better **equipment**: better shoes, better skis, or a better tennis racquet. Even the early Greeks used engineering to make a better discus[1] to throw. However, people want sports to be fair. For this **reason**, sports organizations make rules about athletes, equipment, and the game itself.

2   Nowadays, new **technology** is helping athletes. From high-tech clothing to **artificial** arms and legs, there are many new ways to improve performance. However, many people worry that technology can give some athletes an advantage. It can make competitions unfair. Also, often only wealthier athletes and teams can buy expensive, high-tech equipment. Do we want the best athlete to win, or the athlete with the best equipment to win?

3   The story of high-tech swimsuits shows how technology can make sports unfair. Several years ago, sports engineers **invented** a new material for swimsuits. It has many of the same qualities as shark[2] skin. When swimmers use full-body suits made of this material, they swim faster and float better. The material also sends more oxygen to swimmers' muscles.

4   Companies introduced these new high-tech swimsuits in 2008. Soon after, swimmers using the suits began breaking world swim records at a surprising rate. In the 2008 Beijing Olympic Games, swimmers broke 25 world records. Twenty-three of those swimmers wore the high-tech suits. By comparison, Olympic swimmers broke only eight world records in 2004. Then, in the 2009 World Championships, swimmers broke 43 world records. People knew that the new suits were helping athletes. In January 2010, the Fédération Internationale de Natation (International Swimming Federation, or FINA) **banned** the high-tech suits. Most competitive swimmers were happy about the ban. As one Olympic swimmer said, "Swimming is actually swimming again. It's not who's wearing what suit, who has what material. We're all under the same guidelines[3]."

5   In the two years after the ban, swimmers broke only two world records. Clearly the expensive, high-tech suits were the reason behind the faster swimming times. The suits gave some swimmers an unfair advantage.

---

[1] **discus:** a heavy, flat, round object thrown in a sporting event
[2] **shark:** a large, often dangerous, ocean fish with many sharp teeth

[3] **guidelines:** rules or instructions that are given by an official organization telling you how to do something

6  Better equipment is not always a bad thing, of course. New equipment can certainly be good for a sport. For example, tennis racquets used to be wooden. The heavy rackets could break and cause injuries. In the 1980s, companies introduced new high-tech carbon racquets, which are easier and safer to use. The new racquets have made tennis more enjoyable for the average tennis player. Technology has improved equipment in all sports, from downhill skiing to bicycle racing.

7  The question is this: When does technology create an unfair advantage? In the future, sports engineers may invent an artificial leg that is better than a real leg. Will it be acceptable for competitions? Do high-tech contact lenses give golfers an advantage? Can runners use special shoes that help them run faster while using less **energy**? These questions do not have easy answers. We must make sure that technology does not make sports unfair. However, we should welcome improvements that make sports more enjoyable and safer for all.

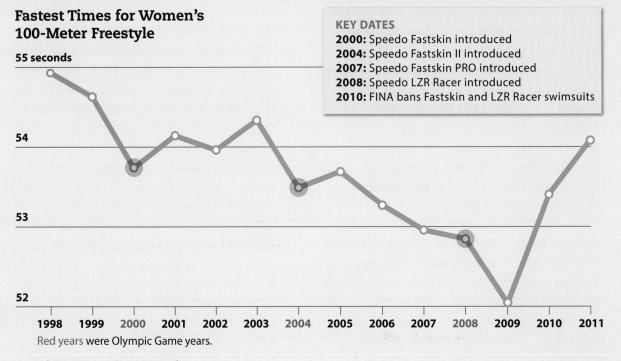

**Fastest Times for Women's 100-Meter Freestyle**

**KEY DATES**
**2000:** Speedo Fastskin introduced
**2004:** Speedo Fastskin II introduced
**2007:** Speedo Fastskin PRO introduced
**2008:** Speedo LZR Racer introduced
**2010:** FINA bans Fastskin and LZR Racer swimsuits

Red years were Olympic Game years.

Source: http://engineeringsport.co.uk

**B. Read one student's notes for the article. Write the correct paragraph number next to each note.**

_6_ a.  Some improvements are good; sports become easier, safer.

_4_ b.  Swimmers broke many new records in 2008–2009; FINA banned suits in 2010.

_1_ c.  Athletes always look for ways to improve performance.

_5_ d.  After ban, swimmers broke few records.

**3** e. Engineers invented new material; like shark skin.

**2** f. Technology can give athletes an advantage.

**7** g. Many questions about technology and sports; no easy answers.

**C. Answer these questions.**

1. Why are some people concerned about technology in sports?

   _unfair advantages. to be fair_

2. What were the advantages of the full-body swimsuits?

   _They swim faster and float better_

3. How did people know that the new swimsuit material gave swimmers an advantage?

   _breaking many records_

4. Who banned swimmers from using the new material in swimsuits?

   _International Swimming Federation (FINA)_

5. What happened to swimming records after the swim organization banned the suits?

   _few records as broken_

6. According to the article, what are some high-tech inventions that may give athletes an advantage in the future?

   _artificial leg, contact lenses, especial shoes_

**D. Read the statements about the graph on page 86. Write *T* (true) or *F* (false). Then correct each false statement to make it true.**

**F** 1. The graph shows the fastest times for women swimmers between 1990 and 2010.

   _98 - 2011_

**F** 2. The slowest time was in 2003, and the fastest time was in 2009.

   _1998_

**F** 3. The fastest time increased by 1.5 minutes in 2009.

   _3 seconds_

___T___ 4. The Speedo Company introduced four different swimsuit designs between 2000 and 2008.

_____

___F___ 5. Overall, times have not decreased between 1998 and 2011.

*Time decreased,*

**E.** **Discuss these questions with a partner or in a group.**

1. Some swimmers were in favor of the new swimsuit material. List three reasons swimmers might be in favor of the material.

2. Do you think it was a good idea to ban the swimsuit material in 2010? Why or why not?

## WRITE WHAT YOU THINK

**A.** **Discuss these questions in a group. Look back at your Quick Write on page 84 as you think about what you learned.**

1. Think of a sport that you enjoy doing or watching. How has technology changed the sport or its equipment? Is the sport safer than it was 50 years ago? Is the sport easier to do?

2. In general, it seems that athletes perform better and are stronger than in the past. Why do you think that is? What are some possible reasons?

**B.** **Go online to watch the video about special high-tech "skinsuits" used by the United States speed skaters in the 2014 Olympic Games in Sochi, Russia. Then check your comprehension.**

| VIDEO VOCABULARY |
| --- |
| **aerodynamic** (*adj.*) designed to move quickly through the air |
| **blame** (*n.*) responsibility for something bad |
| **meltdown** (*n.*) a situation in which something fails in a sudden or dramatic way |
| **venting** (*v.*) strongly expressing a feeling, especially anger |

**C.** **Think about the unit video, Reading 1, and Reading 2 as you discuss these questions. Then choose one question and write a response.**

1. In the Olympic Games, competitions should be fair. Do you think they are? What can make a competition unfair at the Olympics?

2. In addition to money and technology, what else can improve an athlete's performance? In your opinion, what can make the biggest difference?

### Understanding additional information

A dictionary gives you more than just the definition of a word. It also gives you other useful information. For example:

- the pronunciation of the word
- the part of speech
- example sentences to show how to use the word correctly
- other forms of the word

When you read the example sentences, notice which prepositions are used with a particular verb. Notice which nouns are used with a particular adjective. Understanding additional information in a dictionary will help you learn how to use new words correctly.

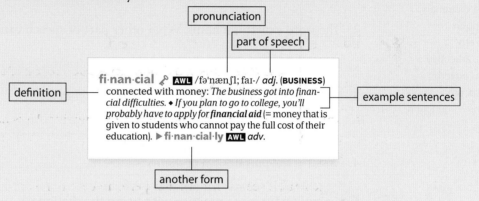

All dictionary entries are from the *Oxford American Dictionary for learners of English* © Oxford University Press 2011.

---

**A.** Read the dictionary entry below. Then answer the questions.

> **com·pete** /kəm'pit/ *verb* [I] **compete (against/with sb) (for sth)** to try to win or achieve something, or to try to be better than someone else: *The world's best athletes compete in the Olympic Games.* ◆ *The teams are competing for the state championship.* ◆ *When they were kids, they always used to compete with each other.* ◆ *They had to compete against several larger companies to get the contract.*

1.  Which prepositions are used with the verb **compete**? _____

2.  Which prepositions are used in these phrases?

    a.  compete _____ or _____ a person

    b.  compete _____ the championship

    c.  compete _____ each other

    d.  compete _____ the Olympic Games

3. Which example sentence shows that *compete* is not just for sports?

_____

4. Using the example sentences as a guide, write two of your own sentences with *compete*.

_____

_____

**Tip** for Success

Be sure you know the abbreviations and meanings for parts of speech in a dictionary.

*n.* noun
*v.* verb
*adj.* adjective
*adv.* adverb
*prep.* preposition
*conj.* conjunction

**B.** Use your dictionary to answer the questions.

1. What part of speech is the word *responsibility*? *responsible*?

_____, _____

2. The word *expert* is a noun. What other part of speech can it be?

_____

3. What parts of speech is the word *profit*? *profitable*?

_____ and _____, _____

4. What is the plural form of *ability*? _____

**iQ** ONLINE **C.** Go online for more practice with using the dictionary.

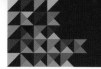

# WRITING

**At the end of this unit, you will write an opinion paragraph about what makes a competition unfair. This paragraph will include specific information from the readings and your own ideas.**

## Writing Skill | Writing an opinion paragraph

In an **opinion paragraph**, you give your ideas about a topic. Writers often introduce their opinions with these phrases:

*I (do not) think (that); I (do not) believe (that); In my opinion; I feel (that)*

> **I do not think** that it is fair for poor teams to compete against wealthy teams.
> **I believe that** players should not be permitted to break the rules.

Writing **Tip**

Phrases that introduce your opinions (*I believe that, I think that*) can make your opinions sound more polite.

In an opinion paragraph, you want to make the reader agree with your opinion, so you need to support your opinion with **reasons** and **supporting details** or **examples**.

> Wealthy teams can sell tickets at high prices because fans want to see the top players in action.
> Second, television stations pay the teams to broadcast their games.
> Third, large companies support the best teams.

Your paragraph should end with a strong **concluding sentence**. Your concluding sentence should restate the topic of your paragraph and your opinion about it.

> For these reasons, I believe that the new equipment is unfair.
> I feel strongly that money creates an unfair advantage in sports.

**A.** **WRITING MODEL** **Read the model opinion paragraph. Then answer the questions on page 92.**

As technology becomes more and more advanced, athletes will soon have contact lenses that do more than correct vision problems. High-tech contact lenses can greatly improve eyesight so that an athlete's eyesight is much stronger than the average person's. This gives an unfair advantage to some athletes. In my opinion, sports organizations ought to have rules against contact lenses in competitions. Eyesight is extremely important in sports like golf and baseball. Athletes have to see objects that are very far away. For this reason, if they have super-vision because of high-tech contact lenses, they will play better than other athletes. We already have reports that this is true. Professional golfers say that high-tech contact lenses have greatly improved their performance. The cost is another reason I am against high-tech contact lenses. These lenses are too expensive for many players. Players who cannot afford them are at a disadvantage. For these reasons, I feel strongly that there must be rules against high-tech contact lenses in some sports.

1. In which sentence does the writer introduce the opinion? What phrase signals the opinion?

   _____

2. Where does the writer give background information about the topic?

   _____

3. What are the two reasons for the writer's opinion?

   _____

4. What phrase signals each reason?

   _____

5. Where does the writer restate the paragraph topic?

   _____

Critical Thinking 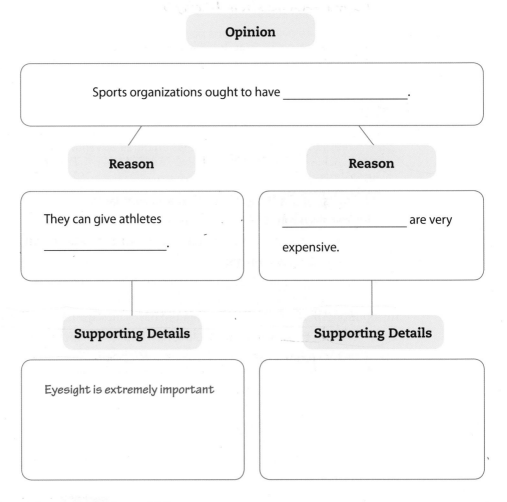 Tip

In Activity B, you have to show your understanding of a reading text by completing a graphic organizer. Showing information using a graphic organizer is a good way to analyze how writers develop their ideas.

**B.** Fill in the graphic organizer with information from the paragraph on page 91.

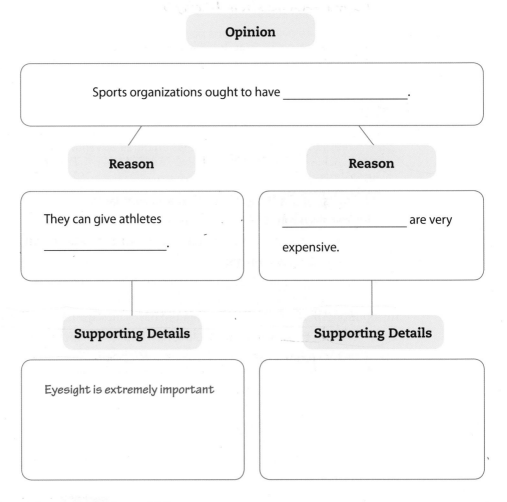

**Opinion**

Sports organizations ought to have _____.

**Reason**

They can give athletes _____.

**Reason**

_____ are very expensive.

**Supporting Details**

Eyesight is extremely important

**Supporting Details**

**C.** Choose a topic for an opinion paragraph. Then plan your writing. Make a graphic organizer similar to the one in Activity B. Fill it in with ideas for your paragraph. Include reasons, details, and examples.

Topic A: What sport do you think is the best for a young child to learn?

Topic B: Some parents encourage students to specialize in just one sport at a very early age. They want their children to be very skilled and competitive. Is this a good idea?

**D.** Write sentences to use in your paragraph.

1. Write a sentence introducing your opinion. Remember, this is usually not the first sentence in the paragraph.

   _____

2. Write a concluding sentence. It can restate your opinion in different words.

   _____

**E.** Write an opinion paragraph. Use your graphic organizer from Activity C and your sentences from Activity D.

 **F.** Go online for more practice with opinion paragraphs.

## Grammar  Modals

One way to give your opinion is to use the **modals** *should, should (not),* and *ought to.*

> Professional athletes **should have** lower salaries.
> Coaches **ought to follow** the rules.
> I believe that disabled athletes **should not compete** against
>    able-bodied athletes.

Note that *ought not* is rarely used.

To make a very strong statement of your opinion, you can use *must* and *must not.*

> Officials **must allow** disabled athletes to participate in the Olympic Games.
> We **must not** let sports be unfair in our schools.

**A.** Look at the paragraph on page 91. Circle the modals *ought to* and *must*.

**B.** Complete the first part of these sentences using *should, should not,* or *ought to.* Then finish the sentence with your own ideas. Use each modal at least once. Then compare and discuss your answers with a partner.

*[handwritten margin note: 2 must not ¿ (definitivo)]*

1. I think that children ___should not___ compete in very competitive sports because ___they are too young___.

2. Athletes ___should not___ take drugs to improve their performance because ___it is unfair___.

3. I believe that there ___ought to___ be a limit on salaries for professional soccer players because ___it is unfair___.

4. In my opinion, athletes in schools ___should___ get good grades because ___they want to earn scholarships___.

**C.** Look back at your opinion paragraph in Activity E on page 93. Underline the modals. If there are no modals, rewrite some of your sentences to include modals.

 **D.** Go online for more practice with modals.

**E.** Go online for the grammar expansion.

---

## Unit Assignment | Write an opinion paragraph

**UNIT OBJECTIVE** ▶▶▶▶ In this assignment, you will write an opinion paragraph. As you prepare your paragraph, think about the Unit Question, "What makes a competition unfair?" Use information from Reading 1, Reading 2, the unit video, and your work in this unit to support your opinion paragraph. Refer to the Self-Assessment checklist on page 96.

 Go to the Online Writing Tutor for a writing model and alternate Unit Assignments.

# PLAN AND WRITE

**A.** **BRAINSTORM** Complete the activities.

1. What makes a competition unfair? Brainstorm a list of ideas.

_____

_____

_____

2. Circle two or three of the best ideas on your list.

**B.** **PLAN** Discuss your ideas from Activity A in a group. Then write your opinions as a topic sentence for your paragraph and complete the graphic organizer with your reasons and supporting details.

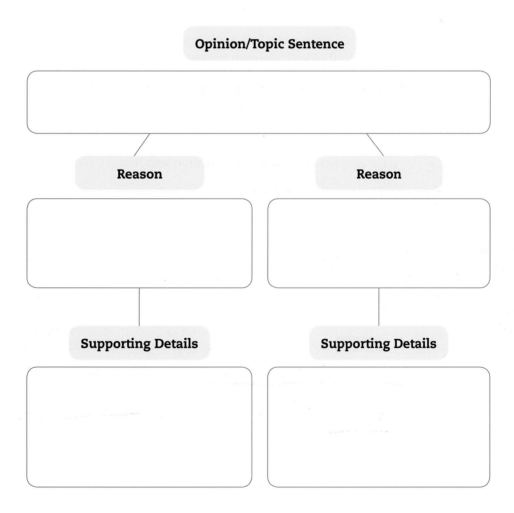

**Opinion/Topic Sentence**

**Reason**

**Reason**

**Supporting Details**

**Supporting Details**

**C.** **WRITE** Use your **PLAN** notes to write your opinion paragraph. Go to *iQ Online* to use the Online Writing Tutor.

1. Include phrases from the Writing Skill on page 91 to introduce your opinions. Use the modals *should (not)*, *ought to*, and *must (not)* to give your opinion. Be sure that your paragraph ends with a strong concluding sentence.

2. Look at the Self-Assessment checklist to guide your writing.

## REVISE AND EDIT

**A.** **PEER REVIEW** Read your partner's paragraph. Then go online and use the Peer Review worksheet. Discuss the review with your partner.

Writing **Tip**

Remember to begin your paragraph with some background information about the topic. Then introduce your opinion. See how the writer did this in the opinion paragraph in Activity A, on page 91.

**B.** **REWRITE** Based on your partner's review, revise and rewrite your opinion paragraph.

**C.** **EDIT** Complete the Self-Assessment checklist as you prepare to write the final draft of your opinion paragraph. Be prepared to hand in your work or discuss it in class.

| SELF-ASSESSMENT | | |
|:---:|:---:|:---|
| Yes | No | |
| ☐ | ☐ | Do you support your opinion with reasons, supporting details, and examples? |
| ☐ | ☐ | Underline any modals in your paragraph. Do you use the base form of verbs after modals? |
| ☐ | ☐ | Is each word used correctly? Check a dictionary if you are not sure. |
| ☐ | ☐ | Does the opinion paragraph include vocabulary from the unit? |
| ☐ | ☐ | Did you check the paragraph for punctuation, spelling, and grammar? |

**D.** **REFLECT** Go to the Online Discussion Board to discuss these questions.

1. What is something new you learned in this unit?

2. Look back at the Unit Question—What makes a competition unfair? Is your answer different now than when you started the unit? If yes, how is it different? Why?

# TRACK YOUR SUCCESS

**Circle the words you have learned in this unit.**

**Nouns**
advantage 🔑
championship
effect 🔑
energy 🔑 AWL
equipment 🔑 AWL
limit 🔑

performance 🔑
reason 🔑
solution 🔑
technology 🔑 AWL

**Verbs**
ban 🔑
compete 🔑

include 🔑
invent 🔑

**Adjectives**
artificial 🔑
financial 🔑 AWL

🔑 Oxford 3000™ words
AWL Academic Word List

**Check (✓) the skills you learned. If you need more work on a skill, refer to the page(s) in parentheses.**

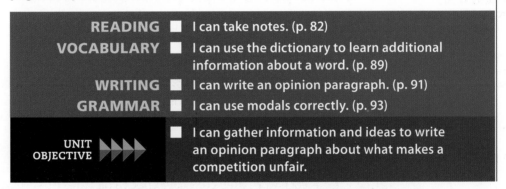

| | |
|---|---|
| **READING** ☐ | I can take notes. (p. 82) |
| **VOCABULARY** ☐ | I can use the dictionary to learn additional information about a word. (p. 89) |
| **WRITING** ☐ | I can write an opinion paragraph. (p. 91) |
| **GRAMMAR** ☐ | I can use modals correctly. (p. 93) |
| **UNIT OBJECTIVE** ▶▶▶▶ ☐ | I can gather information and ideas to write an opinion paragraph about what makes a competition unfair. |

READING ▶ skimming
VOCABULARY ▶ using the dictionary
WRITING ▶ unity in a paragraph
GRAMMAR ▶ comparative and superlative adjectives

**UNIT QUESTION**

# What makes a family business successful?

**A** Discuss these questions with your classmates.

1. Do you know anyone who owns a family business? What kind of business is it? Do you think it is successful?

2. Look at the photo. Who are the people? What can make this type of business successful?

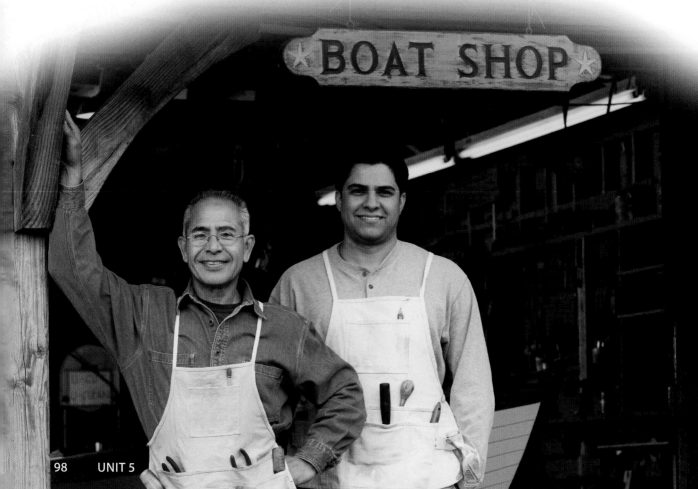

**◉) B** Listen to *The Q Classroom* online. Then answer
these questions.

1. According to Sophy, why is her uncle's business
   successful?

2. Do you think family members are better employees?
   Why or why not?

**iQ** ONLINE **C** Go online to watch the video about a family business that makes zippers.
Then check your comprehension.

**founded** *(v.)* began

**asserted** *(v.)* said that something is true

**come in** *(phr. v.)* finish

**open and shut case** *(phr. n.)* a strong
argument in favor of something

VIDEO VOCABULARY

**iQ** ONLINE **D** Go to the Online Discussion Board
to discuss the Unit Question
with your classmates.

**E** Look at the photos. Match the letter of the photo with the correct quotation. Then discuss the meaning of each quotation with your classmates.

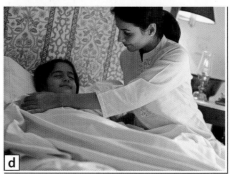

*B* **1.** The family that plays together, stays together. — *Common proverb*

*A* **2.** True happiness is three generations living under one roof.
— *Chinese proverb*

*C* **3.** A man should never neglect his family for business. — *Walt Disney*

*D* **4.** It's more important to know where your children are tonight than where your ancestors were a hundred years ago. — *Anonymous*

**F** Discuss these questions with a partner.

**1.** Do you know any families that have three generations (children, parents, grandparents) living in the same house? How do they get along?

**2.** Do you know any people who put their work before their families? How does this affect the families?

# READING

## READING 1 | Family Unity Builds Success

**UNIT OBJECTIVE**

You are going to read a magazine article about a successful family business. Use the article to gather information and ideas for your Unit Assignment.

## PREVIEW THE READING

 **for Success**

When you read a new word, remember to use the context of the sentence to help you figure out the meaning.

**A. VOCABULARY** Here are some words from Reading 1. Read their definitions. Then complete each sentence.

> **corporation** (*noun*) a big company
>
> **courage** (*noun*) 🔑 not being afraid or not showing that you are afraid when you do something dangerous or difficult
>
> **design** (*verb*) 🔑 to plan and develop how something will look
>
> **expand** (*verb*) 🔑 to become bigger, or make something become bigger
>
> **expert** (*noun*) 🔑 a person who knows a lot about something
>
> **manage** (*verb*) 🔑 to control someone or something
>
> **strength** (*noun*) 🔑 a good quality or ability that someone or something has
>
> **unity** (*noun*) a situation in which people are working together or in agreement

🔑 Oxford 3000™ words

1. Nawaf and Khalid showed a lot of _____courage_____ when they left their country to open a business in France.

2. We hired an architect to help us _____design_____ our new home.

3. Mr. Gibbs is a(n) _____expert_____ on restaurant management. He has managed restaurants for 20 years and has written a book on the subject.

4. The Smiths have a strong sense of _____unity_____ in their family. They always take care of each other.

5. Our business only has six employees now, but we think it will _____expand_____ a lot over the next few years.

6. Turki's greatest _____strength_____ is his ability to keep a positive attitude when times are difficult.

7. Ford, a car company, is an extremely large _corporation_.

8. Mr. Lee is a great teacher. I don't know how he can _manage_ all of those children.

**B.** Go online for more practice with the vocabulary.

**C.** **PREVIEW** Look at the images in Reading 1. What kind of business do you think the article is about? Use the chart below to think of some advantages and disadvantages of working with family members in this type of business.

| Advantages | Disadvantages |
|---|---|
|  |  |

**Writing** **Tip**

When you are writing, try to think of other points of view. Write your own idea, but also think about what someone else might think. Try to use some other ideas as well.

**D.** **QUICK WRITE** Would you open a family business? Write a short paragraph to answer the question. Use your chart from Activity C to describe the advantages and disadvantages of working in a family business. Be sure to use this section for your Unit Assignment.

## Reading Skill  Skimming

**Skimming** is reading a text quickly to get the general idea of what it is about. Skimming is useful when you read a newspaper or magazine, read online, or take a test. When you do research, you skim an article to see if it will be useful. When you skim, use these tips.

- Read the title.
- Quickly read the first sentence of each paragraph.
- Move your eyes quickly through the text.
- Do not read every sentence or every word.
- If the text is short, read the first and last sentence of each paragraph.

**A.** Take one minute to skim Reading 1 on pages 103–104. As you skim, underline the first sentence of each paragraph.

**B.** Write what you can remember about the reading.

**C.** Take one minute to skim Reading 2 on pages 109–110. Then look at the chart below. Check (✓) which reading has information about each topic.

| Which reading has information about... | Reading 1 | Reading 2 |
|---|:---:|:---:|
| 1. a family that owned a newspaper | ☐ | ☑ |
| 2. a restaurant business | ☐ | ☐ |
| 3. family businesses in the United States | ☐ | ☐ |
| 4. a family business owned by immigrants | ☐ | ☐ |
| 5. difficulties with family businesses | ☐ | ☐ |

 **D.** Go online for more practice with skimming.

## WORK WITH THE READING

**A.** Read the magazine article and gather information about what makes a family business successful.

# Family Unity Builds Success

1  When her five daughters were young, Helene An always told them that there was **strength** in **unity**. To show this, she held up one chopstick, representing one person. Then she easily broke it into two pieces. Next, she tied several chopsticks together, representing a family. She showed the girls it was hard to break the tied chopsticks. This lesson about family unity stayed with the daughters as they grew up.

2  Helene An and her family own a multi-million-dollar restaurant business in California. However, when Helene and her husband Danny left their home in Vietnam in 1975, they didn't have much money. They moved their family to San Francisco. There they joined Danny's mother, who owned a small Italian sandwich shop. The Ans began with only a small idea and never dreamed of the success they have today.

3  Soon after the Ans' arrival in the United States, Helene and her mother-in-law, Diana, changed the sandwich shop into a small Vietnamese restaurant. They named it Green Dragon, which symbolizes good luck in Vietnamese. The restaurant was very popular, and they **expanded** from 20 seats to 70. The five daughters helped in the restaurant when they were young. Their mother told them that they all had to work hard to reach their goals and make their family stronger. Helene did not want her daughters to always work in the family business because she thought it was too hard.

4  Eventually the girls all graduated from college and went away to work for themselves, but one by

**A Vietnamese sandwich**

one, the daughters returned to work in the family business. They opened new restaurants in San Francisco and in Beverly Hills, a wealthy area in Los Angeles. The daughters chose new names and styles for their restaurants. Over the years, some ideas were successful, but others were not. Even though family members sometimes disagreed with each other, they worked together to make the business successful. Daughter Elizabeth explains, "Our mother taught us that to succeed we must have unity, and to have unity we must have peace. Without the strength of the family, there is no business. So even when we don't agree, we are willing to try a new idea."

5 Their expanding business became a large **corporation** in 1996, with three generations of Ans working together. Helene is the **expert** on cooking. Helene's husband Danny An is good at making decisions. Their daughter Hannah is good with computers. Hannah's husband Danny Vu is good at thinking of new ideas and doing research. Hannah's sister Elizabeth is the family designer. She **designs** the insides of the restaurants. Their sister Monique is good at **managing**. Elizabeth says, "If you're going to work as a family, you have to know what you're good at. We work well together because we have different strengths." Even the grandchildren help out.

6 Now the Ans' corporation makes more than $20 million each year. Although they began with a small restaurant, they had big dreams, and they worked together. Now they are a big success. Helene says, "In Vietnam, I didn't have to do anything for myself. Here, I've had to do everything. But I was never unhappy because every day I could see all the members of my family, and that gave me **courage** to do more. This has been our greatest fortune[1], to work together as a family."

[1] **fortune:** good luck

**B. Circle the answer to each question.**

1. What is the main idea of paragraph 1?
   a. Family businesses can have problems.
   b. There is strength in working together as a family.
   c. Only family businesses are successful.

2. What is the main idea of paragraph 5?
   a. By 1996, the An family business was a large corporation.
   b. Different family members have strengths that help the business.
   c. The family members didn't know what they were good at.

3. What is the main idea of the entire article?
   a. Any family can become a big success.
   b. Family members have different strengths.
   c. A family that has unity can be successful.

## C. Write the correct paragraph number next to each detail.

_4_ a. After college, the daughters returned to work in the family business.

_6_ b. The Ans' company makes more than $20 million each year.

_2_ c. Helene and Danny An left Vietnam in 1975 with little money.

_5_ d. The business became a corporation in 1996.

_3_ e. The An daughters worked in the restaurant when they were young.

## D. Match each family member with the correct skill.

_e_ 1. Helene      a. managing

_c_ 2. Danny An      b. design

_d_ 3. Hannah      c. making decisions

_f_ 4. Danny Vu      d. computers

_a_ 5. Monique      e. cooking

_b_ 6. Elizabeth      f. new ideas and research

## E. Answer these questions.

1. Why didn't Helene An want her daughters to work in the family business?

She _____

2. Were all of the family's new ideas successful?

No everythingh _____

3. According to Helene An, there was one thing that the family needed for success. What was it?

Unity _____

4. According to Elizabeth, why do the family members work well together?

Each person have different strength

5. According to Helene An, what is the best thing about her family's situation?

She see the family every day.

**F.** Number these events in the order in which they occurred.

_6_ **a.** The business became a corporation.

_7_ **b.** The company made more than $20 million per year.

_3_ **c.** The family changed their small shop into a larger restaurant.

_1_ **d.** The family left their home in Vietnam without much money.

_2_ **e.** The family moved to San Francisco.

_4_ **f.** The daughters finished their education and started their own jobs.

_5_ **g.** The daughters came back to work with their parents.

**iQ** ONLINE **G.** Go online to read *Who Is in Your Family?* and check your comprehension.

# WRITE WHAT YOU THINK

**A.** Ask and answer these questions with a partner.

1. The An family members respect each other. How does this help them have a successful business?

2. What strengths do you have that help you when working in a group?

**B.** Choose one of the questions and write a response. Use supporting examples. Look back at your Quick Write on page 102 as you think about what you learned.

Question: _____

My Response: _____

_____

_____

# READING 2 | The Challenge of Running a Family Business

UNIT OBJECTIVE ▶▶▶▶ You are going to read a textbook article about the difficulties of owning a family business. Use the article to gather information and ideas for your Unit Assignment.

## PREVIEW THE READING

**Vocabulary Skill Review**

In Unit 4, you used the dictionary to learn about pronunciation, parts of speech, and related forms of words. Use your dictionary to check on the pronunciation and related word forms of *challenge, enthusiasm, realistic,* and *responsibility.*

**A.** **VOCABULARY** Here are some words from Reading 2. Read the sentences. Circle the answer that best matches the meaning of each <u>underlined</u> word or phrase.

1. For many parents, communicating with their teenage children can be a big <u>challenge</u>. At this age children may not want to talk to their parents about their problems.
   a. an exciting event
   b. a difficult thing that makes you try hard

2. Mario will be a great sports reporter because of his great <u>enthusiasm</u> for sports.
   a. difficulty with something
   b. strong feeling of liking something

3. My children <u>depend on</u> me to drive them to school.
   a. need someone to provide something
   b. help someone

4. Oliver's store isn't making much money. He's worried that it's going to <u>fail</u>.
   a. be unsuccessful
   b. break the law

5. Ahmed's <u>goals</u> for the future do not include joining the family business.
   a. things that you want to do
   b. subjects that you study

6. Paula is spending more time with her friends and less time studying. Her father is worried about her change in <u>lifestyle</u>.
   a. the way that you dress
   b. the way that you live

7. My grandmother will <u>pass down</u> her jewelry to my mother.
   a. give something to a younger person
   b. create something

🔑 Oxford 3000™ words

8. Jack still thinks he's going to become a basketball star. He needs to be more <u>realistic</u> about his career.

    a. interested and excited

    (b) understanding what is possible

9. Carl's <u>responsibility</u> at home is taking out the garbage. His brother has to set the table for dinner.

    a. things that you must buy

    (b.) jobs or duties that you must do

10. My cousin has a <u>talent</u> for writing. She writes wonderful stories.

    (a.) natural skill or ability

    b. thing you want

**B. Go online for more practice with the vocabulary.**

**Tip** for Success

When you are skimming a text, use a pencil tip to help your eyes move quickly across the text, or place a piece of paper under each line as your read. This will help you avoid stopping to read every word.

**C. PREVIEW** Skim the reading. Which paragraph gives an example of an actual family business?

**D. QUICK WRITE** What problems might owners of a family business face? Write a few sentences before you read. Be sure to use this section for your Unit Assignment.

# WORK WITH THE READING

**A.** Read the article about the challenges of running a family business and gather information about what makes a family business successful.

### The Challenge of Running a Family Business

1  In the United States, families own about 85 percent of all businesses. However, less than 30 percent of these companies last more than 20 years. The companies **fail**, and the owners can't **pass down** the family businesses to their sons and daughters. Why is it so difficult for family businesses to survive?

2  One reason may be changing times. Fifty years ago, many families owned local grocery stores. But today, small family-owned stores cannot compete with large supermarket chains. Today, most Mom and Pop stores[1] are a thing of the past[2]. The way of life is another **challenge** in a family business. A successful company requires hard work and long hours. Younger generations may not want this **lifestyle**. They may want more freedom. In addition, sons and daughters may not have the same **enthusiasm** for the business as their parents.

The Wall Street Journal

3  A successful family business **depends on** the family's strengths and **talents**. However, families also bring their weaknesses and personal problems to the workplace. Many families do not communicate well, and they are not good at solving problems together. These challenges often cause businesses to fail. According to Professor Randel Carlock, these problems are common. He says, "Being part of a family is very difficult. Being part of a family business is even more difficult." Love is important in a family, but love is not enough to run a family business. The business must achieve financial success.

4  The Bancroft family is an interesting example. For 105 years, the Bancroft family owned *The Wall Street Journal*. It is one of the most famous newspapers in the United States. But there were many family problems. They did not communicate well, and they disagreed about many things. One person said that they couldn't even agree on where to go for lunch! The younger family members wanted the business to be more profitable. The older members thought the quality of the paper was more important than making money. In addition, the family let people outside of

Less than 30 percent of family businesses last more than 20 years.

[1] **Mom and Pop stores:** stores owned by a family or individual, not a corporation
[2] **thing of the past:** something that no longer exists

the family manage the newspaper. They did not take part in many important decisions. Finally, in 2007, all 33 of the Bancroft family owners agreed to sell the company. Although the business had lasted several generations, the Bancrofts eventually had to sell their company because they did not manage it well. In the end, many of their family relationships suffered.

5    Many families dream of passing down their businesses to the next generation, but this requires careful planning and preparation. Good management is a key to success. All employees, especially family members, need to have clear **responsibilities**. Family business owners need to think about how decisions are made. Also, they should be **realistic** about the dreams and **goals** of the younger generation. Family businesses can be successful because of strong family ties[3]. But to succeed for more than one generation, families need to manage their businesses carefully.

[3] **ties:** something that connects you with other people

**B.** **Read the statements and write _T_ (true) or _F_ (false). Then correct each false statement to make it true.**

_F_ 1. Fifty percent of family businesses are passed down to the next generation.

    85 percent.

_F_ 2. Most family businesses change and adjust to new ideas and products.

    Few family businesses change.

_F_ 3. Most owners of family businesses don't want to pass down the businesses to their sons and daughters.

    They do want to pass down the businesses.

_F_ 4. According to the article, love is enough to run a family business.

    Love is not enough to run a family success.

_F_ 5. The Bancroft family managed their newspaper by themselves.

    Let people outside managed the newspaper.

**C.** **Look back at paragraph 1 in Reading 2 to find the missing information for the sentences below.**

1. In the United States, families own about 85 percent of all businesses.

    However, less than 30 percent of these businesses last more than

    20 years.

2. Write each phrase from the box in the correct section of the pie charts.

Businesses that are not family-owned

Family-owned businesses

Family-owned businesses that last more than 20 years

Family-owned businesses that fail within 20 years

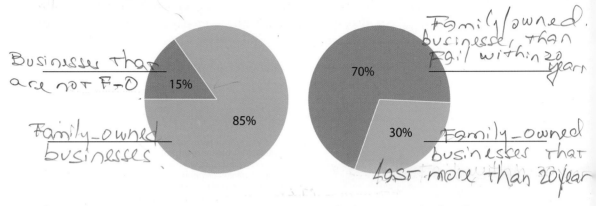

*[handwritten annotations:]* Businesses that are not F-O · Family-owned businesses · Family owned Businesses than Fail within 20 years · Family-owned businesses that last more than 20 year

Pie chart 1: 15%, 85%
Pie chart 2: 70%, 30%

**D.** Look back at Reading 2 on pages 109–110 to find reasons why family businesses fail. Write two of the reasons below. Then compare your answers with a partner.

_____

_____

# WRITE WHAT YOU THINK

**A.** Discuss these questions in a group. Look back at your Quick Write on page 108 as you think about what you learned.

1. What are some advantages to working in the same business with your family? What are some disadvantages?

2. Why do you think most small businesses fail in the first few years?

**Critical Thinking** Tip

Activity B asks you to think about a video and two articles as you answer questions. This is called **synthesizing**. When you **synthesize**, you combine ideas from several sources as you develop your own ideas.

**B.** Think about the unit video, Reading 1, and Reading 2 as you discuss these questions. Then choose one question and write a response.

1. What are the keys to making a family business successful?

2. What differences do you see in the three family businesses: the Feibushes (zippers), the Ans (restaurants), and the Bancrofts (newspapers)? Why do you think that the An family was successful but the Bancroft family had to sell their business?

### Understanding grammatical information in the dictionary

When you look up a word in the dictionary, pay attention to the grammatical information. In addition to the part of speech, an entry may also tell you:

- if a noun is countable (C) or uncountable (U)
- if the plural of a noun has an irregular form
- if an adjective or adverb has an irregular comparative form
- if a verb has an irregular form

Looking up and understanding grammatical information about a new word helps you use the word correctly.

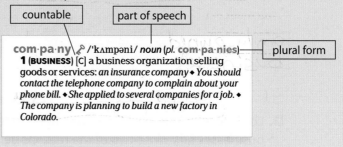

countable    part of speech    plural form

**com·pa·ny** /ˈkʌmpəni/ *noun* (*pl.* **com·pa·nies**)
**1** (BUSINESS) [C] a business organization selling goods or services: *an insurance company* ◆ *You should contact the telephone company to complain about your phone bill.* ◆ *She applied to several companies for a job.* ◆ *The company is planning to build a new factory in Colorado.*

All dictionary entries are from the *Oxford American Dictionary for learners of English* © Oxford University Press 2011.

**A.** Use your dictionary to answer these questions.

1. Which words are uncountable? Circle them.

| | | |
|---|---|---|
| advantage | happiness | participant |
| advice | information | planet |
| darkness | luggage | police |
| furniture | news | traffic |

2. What is the plural form of each of these nouns?

   a. analysis ___analysis___     c. child ___children___

   b. cactus ___cactus___     d. life ___lifes___

3. What is the simple past form of each of these phrases?

   a. break down _____

   b. burst into _____

   c. shine at _____

 **B.** Go online for more practice with using the dictionary.

# WRITING

**UNIT OBJECTIVE** At the end of this unit, you will write a plan for a family business. This plan will include specific information from the readings and your own ideas.

## Writing Skill    Unity in a paragraph

A paragraph is a group of sentences about a single idea. The topic sentence introduces the audience to the topic. The concluding sentence may summarize the contents of the paragraph. The sentences in the middle provide details to support the main idea. All of the sentences in the paragraph should be about the same main idea. The sentences should be closely related to each other. This gives the paragraph **unity**—all parts of the paragraph work together to support a single main idea.

Sentences or ideas that are <u>not</u> closely related to the main idea are irrelevant—they do not help explain and support the main idea.

To be relevant, your sentences should:

- be <u>directly</u> related to the main idea
- support the main idea, but not repeat it
- give new information or details that support the main idea
- not introduce an entirely new main idea that is different from the topic sentence

When you edit your writing, remove or change any sentences that are irrelevant. If all the sentences clearly contribute to the main idea, your paragraph will have unity.

**Transition words** also keep your paragraphs unified. Transition words help your paragraphs read smoothly from one sentence to the next. They help the reader see the connections between ideas. Transition words can serve several purposes:

**to add:** *and, besides, finally, further, too, next, in addition, also, first (second, etc.)*

**to give an example:** *for example, for instance*

**to emphasize:** *definitely, obviously, always, certainly*

Use transition words to help keep your paragraphs unified.

**A.** **WRITING MODEL** Read the model paragraph. Then answer the questions.

Many workers today have different options about how and where they work. Thanks to technology, some people can live far away from their offices and work from home. Computers and the Internet make it possible for individuals to telecommute—that is, to use the telephone and technology to get their work done without being in the office. In addition, since most computers now have microphones and video cameras, it is easy to have a meeting even when people are far away from each other. Now if someone gets

*(handwritten annotations: "Main Idea (Topic Sentences)" above the first sentence, with "Many workers today have different options about how and where they work." circled)*

a new job, they may not have to move to a new city. Maybe in the future, no one will work in an office at all. Everyone will work from home.

1. Circle the topic sentence that has the main idea.

2. How many supporting sentences are there? Underline them.

3. Are all of the sentences in the paragraph about the same idea?

**B.** **WRITING MODEL** **Read the model paragraphs. Circle the main idea. Then cross out any unrelated sentences that don't help support the main idea.**

1. People from the same family are sometimes quite different. Perhaps the father is usually quiet, while the mother is likely to be noisy. Brothers and sisters can also have very different personalities. Two brothers might both be very funny. There can also be large differences in appearance. Some family members may be tall, while others are short. Perhaps they have similar hair or faces. As you can see, family members may not be very similar at all.

2. There are many keys to running a successful business. First, it is important to be sure that your business is in the right location. You want enough people to come and shop there. Many businesses fail in their first few years because they are in a poor location. A good advertising plan can also be helpful. Besides that, you must be sure that the prices are not too high or too low. If you lose money, you can borrow from a bank. My uncle did that during the first two years of his business. If you do everything right, your business can be a big success.

**C.** **Use the transition words from the box to complete the paragraph. For some sentences, there is more than one correct transition word.**

| finally | for instance | next |
| first | in addition | obviously |

If you want to start a new school, there are several things you must consider. _____First_____, you need to think about
what age group you will teach. _____next_____ you
must decide on the curriculum—the subject matter that you will teach.
_____For instance_____, will your school teach driving, or will
you teach photography? _____In addition_____, you will need a
place for students to study. _____Obviously_____, you will also
need teachers. _____Finally_____ you need to decide how
everyone will be paid.

**D.** **WRITING MODEL** Read the model paragraph describing a plan for a new school. Then answer the questions.

*Main Idea*

I am going to start a new cooking school in our neighborhood. This new school will be for college graduates who are living away from their families. In our school, we will offer classes in the morning and in the evening to fit different schedules. Also, our classes will teach the easiest and most delicious dishes. In addition, students can study specialized subjects. For example, there will be courses on making soups and on baking. The classes will be taught by experienced cooks from a variety of backgrounds. I will make sure that there are not too many students in any one class. We will get money from wealthy people and companies to help pay for the school. Finally, we will regularly ask experts to give us ideas on how to make the school better. I'm sure that our school will be popular and successful.

1. What is the main idea of the paragraph? _____

2. How many transition words do you see? _____ Circle them.

3. Do all of the ideas help support the main idea? _____

4. What are two additional ideas that the writer could add?

   I will make sure that my school includes cookbooks. Also the students will create their own recipes.

**E.** Brainstorm ideas about a plan for a special new school. What will the school be like? Who will the students be? What will you teach? It might be a school for language, photography, driving, or something else.

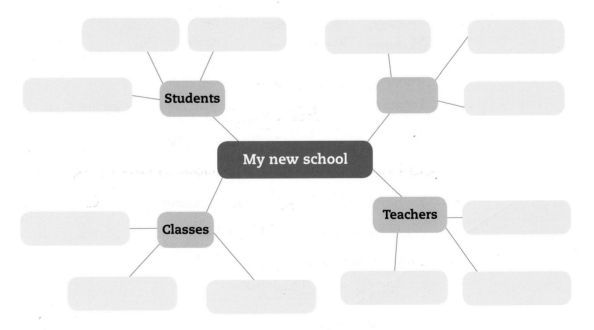

**F.** Write a paragraph describing a special new school. Use ideas from Activity E on page 115. Be sure you have a clear topic sentence and that all of the supporting ideas help unify the paragraph. Use transition words.

**iQ** ONLINE **G.** Go online for more practice with paragraph unity.

## Grammar  Comparative and superlative adjectives

**Comparative adjectives** describe the difference between two things.

For adjectives with one syllable, use *adjective + er*. *Than* often follows comparative adjectives.

| tall | → | taller | The Burj Khalifa is **taller than** Taipei 101. |
| safe | → | safer | |
| big | → | bigger | |

If an adjective ends in one vowel and one consonant, double the consonant, as in *big → bigger*. If the adjective ends in -*e*, just add -*r*.

For most adjectives with two or more syllables, use *more + adjective*.

| common | → | more common |
| traditional | → | more traditional |

For two-syllable adjectives that end in -*le*, add -*r*.

| simple | → | simpler |

For two-syllable adjectives that end in -*y*, change the -*y* to *i* and add -*er*.

| pretty | → | prettier |
| funny | → | funnier |

**Superlative adjectives** describe three or more things.

For most adjectives that have one syllable, use *the + adjective + -est*.

| tall | → | the tallest |
| big | → | the biggest |
| safe | → | the safest |

For two-syllable adjectives that end in -*le*, use *the* and add –*st*.

| simple | → | the simplest |

For two-syllable adjectives that end in -*y*, change the *y* to *i*, use *the*, and add -*est*.

| funny | → | the funniest |

For most adjectives with two or more syllables, add *the + most + adjective*.

| informal | → | the most informal |
| realistic | → | the most realistic |
| traditional | → | the most traditional |

Note: Some adjectives are irregular.

| good | → | better | → | the best |
| bad | → | worse | → | the worst |

**A.** Complete the paragraph with words from the box. Change them into comparative form.

| big | clear | pretty | realistic | safe | simple |

Many of us remember the good old days. Those times were
_____**simpler**_____ and less complicated. In those days, we
                1
felt much _____**safer**_____ in our own neighborhoods. There
                        2
was less pollution, and the sky was _____**clearer**_____. We
                                              3
may even feel that nature was _____**prettier**_____ back then
                                          4
than it is now. As cities have become _____**bigger**_____,
                                                5
those days may be gone forever. Perhaps we all need to be ___**more**
**realistic.**_____ about the future.
        6

**B.** Look at the adjectives in the chart below. Complete the chart with the missing forms of each adjective.

| Adjective | Comparative | Superlative |
|---|---|---|
| healthy | healthier | the healthiest |
| exciting | more exciting | the most exciting |
| close | closer | the closest |
| easy | easier | the easiest |
| good | better | the best |
| calm | calmer | calmest |
| busy | busier | busiest |
| low | lower | lowest |

**C.** Complete each sentence with the correct comparative form of the adjective in parentheses.

1. I'm ____more____ (successful) in school than my brother is.

2. Sandra is ____more____ (responsible) with her money than her younger sister is.

3. Elephants are ____more____ (intelligent) than fish.

4. People in small towns are often ____friendlier____ (friendly) than people in big cities.

5. The subway is ____faster____ (fast) than the bus.

6. Chan's goals for the future are ____more____ (realistic) than Brendan's.

**D.** Complete each sentence with the correct superlative form of the adjective in parentheses and your own opinions. Then discuss your answers with a partner.

1. ____Ice hockey____ is _the most interesting_ (interesting) sport to watch.

2. _____ is _____ (delicious) food in the world.

3. _____ is _____ (beautiful) season of the year.

4. _____ is _____ (difficult) sport to play.

5. _____ is _____ (famous) place in my country.

6. _____ is _____ (successful) company in the world.

**E.** Go online for more practice with comparative and superlative adjectives.

**F.** Go online for the grammar expansion.

In this assignment, you will write a plan for a new family business. Your plan will include information about your new business, the services it will provide, and the jobs that the members of your family will do. As you prepare to write your plan, think about the Unit Question, "What makes a family business successful?" Use information from Reading 1, Reading 2, the unit video, and your work in the unit to support your writing. Refer to the Self-Assessment checklist on page 120.

 Go to the Online Writing Tutor for a writing model and alternate Unit Assignments.

## PLAN AND WRITE

**A.** **BRAINSTORM** Freewrite to brainstorm ideas for your new family business. What are some possible businesses? What items will you sell or what services will you provide? Think about what jobs the members of your family will do. Write down as many ideas as you can.

_____

_____

_____

_____

_____

Writing

When you are writing a plan, don't just think about what you would like to see. Think about your audience. What might readers want to know about your business?

**B.** **PLAN** Review your freewriting. Choose the business you want to write about. Then answer the questions.

1. What kind of business will it be? What kind of product or service will your business provide?

2. Describe the store or service.

3. Who will your customers be?

4. Why will your business be different from others?

5. Which family members will work in your company? What will their jobs be?

6. Why should people come and buy from your company?

7. Why will your business be successful?

**C.** **WRITE** Use your **PLAN** notes to write your plan for a new family business. Go to *iQ Online* to use the Online Writing Tutor.

1. Write your topic sentence first. Make sure the topic sentence introduces the main idea of the paragraph.

2. Be sure to use examples to support your main idea.

3. Be sure that each sentence is relevant and contributes to the main idea.

4. Look at the Self-Assessment checklist to guide your writing.

## REVISE AND EDIT

**A.** **PEER REVIEW** Read your partner's plan. Then go online and use the Peer Review worksheet. Discuss the review with your partner.

**B.** **REWRITE** Based on your partner's review, revise and rewrite your plan.

**C.** **EDIT** Complete the Self-Assessment checklist as you prepare to write the final draft of your plan. Be prepared to hand in your work or discuss it in class.

| SELF-ASSESSMENT | | |
|:---:|:---:|:---|
| **Yes** | **No** | |
| ☐ | ☐ | Do the sentences in your paragraph support the topic sentence? |
| ☐ | ☐ | Do you use transition words to unify the plan and help your ideas flow smoothly? |
| ☐ | ☐ | Underline any comparative or superlative adjectives. Are they in the correct form? |
| ☐ | ☐ | Is each word used correctly? Check a dictionary if you are not sure. |
| ☐ | ☐ | Does the plan include vocabulary from the unit? |
| ☐ | ☐ | Did you check the plan for punctuation, spelling, and grammar. |

**D.** **REFLECT** Go to the Online Discussion Board to discuss these questions.

1. What is something new you learned in this unit?

2. Look back at the Unit Question—What makes a family business successful? Is your answer different now than when you started the unit? If yes, how is it different? Why?

# TRACK YOUR SUCCESS

**Circle the words and phrases you have learned in this unit.**

**Nouns**
challenge 🔑 AWL
corporation AWL
courage 🔑
enthusiasm 🔑
expert 🔑 AWL
goal 🔑 AWL
lifestyle
responsibility 🔑

strength 🔑
talent 🔑
unity

**Verbs**
design 🔑 AWL
expand 🔑 AWL
fail 🔑
manage 🔑

**Adjectives**
realistic 🔑

**Phrasal Verbs**
depend on 🔑
pass down

🔑 Oxford 3000™ words
AWL Academic Word List

**Check (✓) the skills you learned. If you need more work on a skill, refer to the page(s) in parentheses.**

READING ■ I can skim. (p. 102)

VOCABULARY ■ I can use the dictionary to understand grammatical information. (p. 112)

WRITING ■ I can write a paragraph with unified ideas. (p. 113)

GRAMMAR ■ I can use comparative and superlative adjectives correctly. (pp. 116–117)

UNIT OBJECTIVE ▶▶▶▶ ■ I can gather information and ideas to write a plan for a new family business.

READING ▶ identifying the author's purpose
VOCABULARY ▶ using the dictionary
WRITING ▶ describing a process
GRAMMAR ▶ infinitives of purpose

**UNIT QUESTION**

# Do you prefer to get help from a person or a machine?

**A** Discuss these questions with your classmates.

1. What are some of the advantages of getting help from a machine rather than from a person?

2. What are some of the advantages of getting help from a person rather than a machine?

3. Look at the photo. What are the men doing?

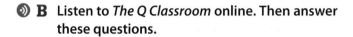

**B** Listen to *The Q Classroom* online. Then answer these questions.

1. Which students prefer to get help from people? Which machines do they dislike?

2. Which students prefer to get help from machines? Which machines do they like?

3. Think of one of the machines that the students mentioned in their discussion. Do you like using that type of machine or technology? Why or why not?

 **C** Go online to watch the video about technology in a restaurant. Then check your comprehension.

**customize** *(v.)* to change something to suit the needs of the owner

**fusion** *(adj.)* cooking that is a mixture of different styles

**hover** *(v.)* to wait near someone in an uncertain manner

**virtual** *(adj.)* made to appear to exist with the use of computer software

VIDEO VOCABULARY

 **D** Go to the Online Discussion Board to discuss the Unit Question with your classmates.

**E** Look at the photos and answer the questions with a partner.

a

Touch-screen ordering kiosk

b

Airport check-in kiosk

c

Supermarket self-service check-out

d

Gas station self-service pump kiosk

1. Which of these self-service machines have you used?

2. How does each of these self-service machines save time?

3. What problems could you have with each machine?

4. Which machine is the most useful? The least useful?

**F** Discuss these questions with your classmates.

1. How many classmates have used each machine in Activity E?

2. What other self-service machines do you and your classmates sometimes use?

## READING 1 | Memo to Restaurant Servers

**UNIT OBJECTIVE** ▶▶▶▶

You are going to read a business memo from a restaurant manager to the servers. Use the memo to gather information and ideas for your Unit Assignment.

## PREVIEW THE READING

**Vocabulary Skill Review**

In Unit 4, you learned to use the dictionary to find additional information about words. Look up the words *benefit* and *blame*. Which prepositions are often used with these words? Which prepositions are used with them if you change the part of speech?

**A.** VOCABULARY Here are some words from Reading 1. Read their definitions. Then complete each sentence.

> **automatically** (*adverb*) 🔑 done in a way (like a machine) that does not require human control
>
> **benefit** (*noun*) 🔑 advantages or good or useful effects of something
>
> **blame** (*verb*) 🔑 to think or say that someone is responsible for something bad that happened
>
> **decrease** (*verb*) 🔑 to become or to make something smaller or less
>
> **error** (*noun*) 🔑 a mistake
>
> **estimate** (*verb*) 🔑 to calculate the approximate size, cost, or amount of something
>
> **interact** (*verb*) to communicate or mix with
>
> **provide** (*verb*) 🔑 to give or supply something to somebody
>
> **stressed** (*adjective*) 🔑 feeling worried or unable to relax
>
> **unique** (*adjective*) 🔑 unlike anything else; being the only one of its type

🔑 Oxford 3000™ words

1. A _benefit_ of having a laptop computer is that you can use it almost anywhere.

2. At the bank, a machine _automatically_ sorts and counts coins.

3. I thought I made many mistakes on the test, but later I found out that I had made only one _error_.

4. I am waiting for prices to _decrease_ before I buy a new laptop.

5. Some people _blame_ the changes in climate on pollution.

6. I _estimate_ that 50 people will be at the meeting?

7. My brother is good with children. He likes to _interact_ with them.

8. Last year I felt very _stress_ about my schoolwork. This year, I have fewer classes, and I feel more relaxed.

9. The school librarians are very helpful. They _provide_ us with a lot of useful information.

10. Instead of a typical cake, Sue made a _unique_ and colorful one.

 **B.** Go online for more practice with the vocabulary.

 **Tip for Success**

Before you read a text, look at the title, photos, and format of the text. Think about what kind of information it might contain.

**C.** **PREVIEW** Quickly read the topic of the memo (in the RE: line) and the questions in paragraph 4 of the memo. What do you think the new technology will be in the restaurant? More than one answer is possible.

☐ Customers will pay their own bills using a credit card at a tablet.

☐ Customers will enter their order at their table using a tablet.

☐ Customers will use their cell phones to order at their table.

**D.** **QUICK WRITE** Think of three ways that restaurants use technology. How is each way useful? How does it make dining more enjoyable for customers? Write your response before you read the article. Be sure to use this section for your Unit Assignment.

## WORK WITH THE READING

**A.** Read the business memo and gather information about getting help from a machine.

Restaurant Z — Memo

DATE:   May 3
TO:     Servers
FROM:   Mark McCormick, Dining Room Manager
RE:     New touch-screen ordering

1   At Restaurant Z, we are known as a cool, trendy place for people who want a special experience. We are always looking for better ways to serve our customers and make their experience **unique**. Next month, we will make

a change so that we can really stand out[1]: touch-screen ordering, also known as "digital dining." You need to know about this new technology.

2  This is how it works: Each table will have its own tablet with a touch screen. Customers can view the menu on the tablet, including descriptions and photos. To start, the customer swipes her credit card and puts in her order by touching the screen. Then the program **automatically** makes suggestions for additional items to order, such as appetizers[2] and drinks. When the customer is ready, she pushes a button to send the order directly to the computer in the kitchen. Won't that make your job as a server easier? All you have to do is bring the food to the table when it's ready! Finally, paying the bill is quick and easy because the customer can do it herself. This exciting new technology will improve our customers' dining experience and increase your tips!

3  Now you may want to know how this change will affect you. Maybe you are afraid of losing your job. Let me assure you: you won't. In fact, you will be able to serve more customers every night! These high-tech tablets not only look cool, they **decrease** the number of tasks you have to do! Hopefully, that means that you can serve more tables without feeling **stressed**.

4  Here are some questions and answers:

**Q:** *What are the **benefits** for me as a server?*

**A:** First of all, with digital dining, customers can order quickly. We will be able to serve more customers in less time. Also, the tablet program will automatically suggest additional items to order. Research shows that when this happens, customers order more. We **estimate** that customer bills will be 15 to 20 percent higher. With more customers ordering more items, you will earn more money in tips. In addition, you won't have to repeat the same information over and over like a robot[3]. Finally, customers can't **blame** you for **errors** in their order—they place their own orders!

**Q:** *Will customers really want to do their own ordering?*

**A:** Yes, I think that most of our customers will love it! If a diner prefers the traditional service, we will **provide** it. But these tablets will be so much fun that everyone will want to use them! The photographs will be fantastic and the descriptions will be mouth-watering. As you know, most of our customers are tech-savvy[4], and they enjoy **interacting** with the latest gadgets[5].

---

[1] **stand out:** to be different
[2] **appetizer:** a small amount of food that you eat as the first part of a meal
[3] **robot:** an automated machine that can do work that a person does
[4] **tech-savvy:** having knowledge and understanding of technology
[5] **gadget:** a small machine or tool

**Q:** *What other features will these tablets have?*

**A:** They'll have entertaining games and high-speed Internet access. Customers can send messages to friends and post photos of themselves at the table.

5 We will be having an employee training session to show you how digital dining works next Tuesday from 9:30–11:00 a.m. I look forward to showing you this fabulous new system!

**B. Circle the answer to each question.**

1. What is the main reason the restaurant is going to use digital dining?
   a. to provide better service to customers
   b. to help servers get larger tips
   c. to be trendy and popular  *(circled)*

2. What was the manager's reason for writing the second section?
   a. to tell how digital dining will increase sales
   b. to explain how digital dining works  *(circled)*
   c. to describe how customers will pay their bills

3. Why does the manager include the question and answer section?
   a. to explain the training servers will receive
   b. to answer questions that customer will ask
   c. to answer questions that servers will have  *(circled)*

4. What is the main idea of the question and answer section?
   a. Someday tablets will replace servers.
   b. Tablets will make servers and customers happy.  *(circled)*
   c. Customers will order more food.

**C. Complete each statement with information from the memo.**

1. The date of the memo is ___May 3___.

2. The restaurant will start using tablets ___next month___.

3. In addition to descriptions of menu items, the tablet will show ___picture, photoshot___.

4. When a customer places an order, the tablet program will recommend ___appetizers and___.

5. Customers' bills will be _____High_____ when they use digital dining.

6. The training meeting will be _____nex tuesday_____.

**D.** Complete the sentences to show the causes and effects or results. Use information from the reading.

| Cause | Effect or result |
|---|---|
| 1. Because the tablet will do many of the servers' tasks, | servers will feel less stressed. |
| 2. _Serve more customers_ | servers will make more money. |
| 3. _Costomers place their own orders_ | customers cannot blame servers for mistakes in their orders. |
| 4. Because the tablet automatically suggests other items to order, | _Customers will order more Food._ |
| 5. Because the tablets will be so much fun to use, | _customers won't mind making their own orders._ |

**E.** Answer these questions.

1. Why does the manager use *we* and *our* in section 1?
   a. because the servers own the restaurant, too
   b. because he wants the servers to feel they are part of a team
   c. because he is also a server

2. Find and underline other uses of *we* and *our* in the memo.

   What sections are they in? _____

3. In section 2, the manager asks, "Won't that make your job as a server easier?" Why does he ask this question?

    a. because he is not sure if the servers will agree with him

    b. because he doesn't know what the servers' answers will be

    (c.) because he expects the servers to agree with him

4. Which sentence from the memo expresses enthusiasm and excitement for this change?

    a. "You need to know about this new technology."

    (b.) "This exciting new technology will improve our customer's dining experience and increase your tips!"

    c. "Maybe you are afraid of losing your job."

5. Find and underline another sentence that expresses enthusiasm. What

    section is it in? _____

 **F.** Go online to read *Voice Recognition Systems* and check your comprehension.

# WRITE WHAT YOU THINK

**A. Discuss these questions in a group.**

1. The manager mentions many of the benefits of the new tablets. What do you think some of the disadvantages or problems might be?

2. At Restaurant Z, who do you think will benefit the most from the new digital dining technology: the customers or the servers?

3. Have you ever used technology like this in a restaurant? If so, describe your experience and tell what happened. If not, would you like to use this technology? Why or why not?

**B. Choose one of the questions and write a response. Look back at your Quick Write on page 126 as you think about what you learned.**

Question: _____

My Response: _____

_____

_____

_____

The **purpose** of a text is the reason the author writes it. For example, the purpose of a newspaper article is to inform or give the reader information about something. The purpose of a letter to the newspaper is usually to express an opinion about something. As you read, look at the words the author uses and ask yourself questions to help you identify the purpose. Here are some questions you can ask yourself as you read:

- Is the author trying to give me information about something?
- Is the author expressing his or her opinion about something?
- Is the author telling me a personal story?
- Is the author trying to make me interested or excited about something?
- Is the author trying to make me laugh?

Identifying the author's purpose can help you better understand the text you are reading.

**A.** Look back at Reading 1 on pages 126–128. What is the author's purpose? Circle two answers.

a. to tell a story

b. to make someone laugh

c. to give information

d. to make someone excited about something

**B.** Read the titles. Look at the words the authors use. Then match each title with the correct purpose.

b 1. "My Embarrassing Adventures with Technology"    a. to tell a story

c 2. "Competitive Sports Are Too Competitive"    b. to make someone laugh

a 3. "My Grandfather's Childhood in Egypt"    c. to express an opinion

e 4. "New Research Shows Birds See More Colors"    d. to make someone interested in something

d 5. "You Can Be Stronger in Two Weeks!"    e. to give information

 **C.** Go online for more practice with identifying the author's purpose.

# READING 2 | I Hate Machines!

 **UNIT OBJECTIVE** You are going to read a blog about how technology can cause problems. A blog is a website with posts or short essays. Use the blog to gather information and ideas for your Unit Assignment.

## PREVIEW THE READING

**Vocabulary Skill Review**

In Unit 5, you learned about grammatical information in the dictionary. Look at the vocabulary on this page and on page 125. Using a dictionary, find out which nouns are countable, which are uncountable, and which can be either countable or uncountable.

**A.** **VOCABULARY** Here are some words from Reading 2. Read their definitions. Then complete each sentence.

> **access** (*noun*) 🔑 a way to enter a place or to use something
> **assist** (*verb*) 🔑 to help someone
> **connection** (*noun*) 🔑 a path of communication for a telephone or Internet
> **eventually** (*adverb*) 🔑 after a long time
> **frustrated** (*adjective*) angry or impatient because you cannot do or achieve what you want to do
> **furious** (*adjective*) very angry   *fury (noun)*
> **install** (*verb*) 🔑 to put a new thing in its place so it is ready to use
> **on hold** (*prepositional phrase*) waiting on the phone to talk to someone or continue a conversation
> **scan** (*verb*) to pass light over a picture or document in order to copy it and put it in the memory of a computer
> **transfer** (*verb*) 🔑 to connect a telephone caller to another person or line

🔑 Oxford 3000™ words

1.  I thought my friends would never come back from the store, but ___eventually___ they did.

2.  Ana called, but I couldn't hear her because my phone had a bad ___connection___.

3.  This key will give you ___access___ to my apartment whenever you want.

4.  At our store the computer specialists ___assist___ customers. It's their job.

5.  I'm not able to answer your question, but I can ___transfer___ you to a manager who can help you.

6.  You don't need to type the price into the cash register. You can just ___scan___ the item with this machine.

7. I tried to register for classes today, but the website didn't work! Now all the classes I want are full. I'm so _____frustrated_____.

8. I hung up after I was ___on hold,___ for 30 minutes.

9. My friend damaged my new car, and then he lied to me about what happened. I was ___furious___!

10. A man came to my apartment to ___install___ my new dishwasher.

**iQ** ONLINE **B. Go online for more practice with the vocabulary.**

**C.** PREVIEW **Blogs are usually informal and personal. Bloggers, people who create blogs, often write about their experiences, giving their opinions about various topics. Look at the title of the blog post in Reading 2. What do you think the reading will be about?**

**D.** QUICK WRITE **Think about the title, "I Hate Machines!" Think about an experience you had with a machine that made you feel the same way. What happened? Write a few sentences about the topic. Be sure to use this section for your Unit Assignment.**

## WORK WITH THE READING

**A. Read the blog and gather information about getting help from a machine.**

# I Hate Machines!

Home          Log in

**Trouble with Technology**                          **About**

TUESDAY, MARCH 2                                        **Links**

1    Recently, I moved to a new apartment right across the street from          **Archives**
my old one. I thought it would be simple to get my phone and DSL[1] line
started. The technician[2] from the phone company came to **install** my               January
telephone line. He said that I would be able to use the Internet on the               February
same line. After he left, I discovered that the phone worked, but the DSL              March

[1] **DSL:** a fast Internet connection through telephone lines.        [2] **technician:** a person who fixes machines
The letters stand for digital subscriber line.

April
May
June
July
August
September
October
November
December

**connection** for the Internet didn't. So I called the phone company. Of course, I didn't get to talk to a real person. Instead, an automated voice recording asked me a lot of questions. Then I had to wait for half an hour to talk to a real person. While I was **on hold**, every few minutes a recording said, "Remember, you can use our convenient website to solve most of your problems." "Arrrrrghh!!" I said to the recording, feeling **frustrated.** "Why do you think I'm calling you? I don't have a connection to the Internet."

2    I finally got to talk to a real person, but then she **transferred** me back into the automated system again. I couldn't get any help. I called a different number, and the person told me to be at my house for a technician to come the next day. I stayed home from work, but nobody came! I called them again. The recording said, "We're sorry, all agents are busy **assisting** other customers. We are unable to take your call." Then the machine hung up on me. Three days later, I received a phone call from them. But again, it wasn't a real person: it was a machine. The voice on the machine said, "We are happy to tell you that you now have Internet **access**." But when I went back to my computer, I still couldn't connect to the Internet. I was **furious**!

3    To make a long story short[3], it took the phone company two weeks to solve my problem. I spent a total of 18 hours at home waiting for workers who never came. I spent eight hours on the phone listening to recordings and machines and waiting on hold. Companies think that these voice-activated systems save us time, but they actually waste it.

4    The telephone isn't the only timesaving technology that drives me crazy[4]. The other day, I went to the supermarket. They had a new self-service checkout system. With this new device, I could **scan** my groceries myself instead of waiting in a checkout line. For some strange reason, these machines seem to hate me. Here's what happened: I scan my item. The computer sits there stupidly and does nothing. **Eventually** it says, "Scan your first item." But I already did! What do I do now? Scan it again and get charged twice? So I put my item in the bag.

5    "Put the item in the bag," says the machine. But I already have!

6    "Put the item in the bag," it says again. So, I take it out and do it again, just to make the machine happy.

7    "Scan the item before putting it in the bag!" shouts the machine while everyone turns to look at me as if I'm an idiot[5]. Grrr!

8    I wish we could go back to the good old days when there were real people to help us. I think I would have been happier living a hundred years ago, before we had all of this timesaving, self-service technology.

[3] **to make a long story short:** to tell something quickly
[4] **drive me crazy:** to make me upset or angry

[5] **as if I'm an idiot:** as if they think that I am stupid

**B. Answer these questions.**

1. What are the two types of automated technology with which the author was frustrated?

   _Automated system / self - service checkout_

2. What was frustrating about his first experience? List three things.

   _He was on hold, the tranferred, No body came at the phone,_

3. How did he feel when he used the self-service checkout? Why?

   _He feel like idiot, because everyone turns to look at him Frustrated and embarase._

4. Why does the writer hate machines? Give at least three reasons.

   _because he waste he's time, The machine not work properly_

5. What is the author's purpose? (Look back at the reading skill on page 131.)

   _the author telling me a personal story!_

6. The blog is humorous. In your opinion, what was the funniest part?

   _#7_

**C. Read the statements. Write _T_ (true) or _F_ (false). Then correct each false statement to make it true.**

_T_ 1. A worker went to the man's house to install a phone line.

_F_ 2. When the man called the telephone company, he never got to talk to a real person.

   _He waiting long Time,_

_F_ 3. It took the phone company three weeks to solve his problem.

   _Two weeks_

_T_ 4. The computer at the supermarket did not work correctly.

_T_ 5. The man thinks he would prefer to have lived in a time before there was technology.

**D.** Look at Reading 2. Identify who said each of the statements. Write *P* if it was a person. Write *C* if it was a computer or an automated voice.

C 1. "Remember, you can use our convenient website to solve most of your problems."

P 2. "Arrrrrghh!!"

P 3. "Why do you think I'm calling you?"

C 4. "We're sorry, all agents are busy assisting other customers."

C 5. "Scan the item before putting it in the bag!"

**E.** Read the statements. Number them to show the correct order.

2 a. I discovered that the phone worked, but the Internet connection didn't.

4 b. The person transferred me to the automated system again.

1 c. A technician from the phone company installed a phone line.

6 d. After two weeks, I finally got my Internet connection.

5 e. I made an appointment, but no one came to fix the connection.

3 f. I called the phone company, waited on hold, and finally spoke with a real person.

# WRITE WHAT YOU THINK

**A.** Discuss these questions in a group. Look back at your Quick Write on page 133 as you think about what you learned.

1. Have you ever been frustrated by new technology? Describe what happened.

2. Do you prefer to interact with people or with self-service machines? Why?

Writing **Tip**

When you write a paragraph in response to a question, begin with a topic sentence. Support your ideas with reasons, supporting details, and examples. End with a strong concluding sentence.

**B.** Think about the unit video, Reading 1, and Reading 2 as you discuss these questions. Then choose one question and write a response.

1. Think of a new type of self-service technology. What are the disadvantages or problems?

2. What is your favorite type of self-service technology? Describe what it is and why you like it.

### Words with more than one meaning

Many words have more than one meaning, or definition, even if they are spelled and pronounced the same way. Using a dictionary can help you identify the correct meaning of a new word. If a word has two definitions that are the same part of speech (*noun*, *verb*, *adjective*, *adverb*), they will likely appear under the same entry in the dictionary. If the two meanings are different parts of speech, they might appear under different entries in the dictionary.

**light¹** /laɪt/ *noun* **1** [C, U] the energy from the sun, a lamp, etc. that allows you to see things: *a beam/ray of light* ◆ *the light of the sun* ◆ *The light was too bad for us to read by.* **2** [C] something that produces light, for example an electric lamp: *Suddenly, all the lights came on/went out.* ◆ *the lights of the city in the distance* ◆ *a neon light* ◆ *That car's lights aren't on.* ◆ *Please switch the lights off before you leave.*

**light²** /laɪt/ *adj.*
> **NOT DARK 1** having a lot of light: *In the summer it's still light at 9 o'clock.* ◆ *a light room* **ANT dark**
> **OF A COLOR 2** pale in color: *a light blue sweater* **ANT dark**
> **NOT HEAVY 3** not of great weight: *Carry this bag – it's the lightest.* ◆ *I've lost weight – I'm five pounds lighter than I used to be.* ◆ *light clothes* (= for summer) **ANT heavy**

You can improve your vocabulary by using a dictionary to look up words with more than one meaning.

All dictionary entries are from the *Oxford American Dictionary for learners of English* © Oxford University Press 2011.

**A.** Use your dictionary to find the different definitions of the words below. Then write the definition and the sentence that uses the word in context. Compare your answers with a partner.

1. light

   Definition 1: _the energy from the sun, a lamp, etc._

   Sentence: _The light was too low for us to see._

   Definition 2: _something that produces light, for example an electric lamp_

   Sentence: _Suddenly, all the lights came on._

   Definition 3: _____

   Sentence: _____

   Definition 4: _____

   Sentence: _____

**Rowing**

**2.** row

Definition 1: _____

Sentence: _____

Definition 2: _____

Sentence: _____

**3.** tip

Definition 1: _____

Sentence: _____

Definition 2: _____

Sentence: _____

Definition 3: _____

Sentence: _____

**4.** bank

Definition 1: _____

Sentence: _____

Definition 2: _____

Sentence: _____

Definition 3: _____

Sentence: _____

**Tip** for Success

Sometimes words with more than one meaning are spelled the same way, but they are pronounced differently. Pay attention to the different pronunciations for the different meanings of *record* and *wind*.

**B.** Work with a partner. Look up the words *record* and *wind* in the dictionary. Answer the questions below.

**1.** How many definitions are there for the word *record*? ____

**2.** How many of the definitions did you already know? ____

**3.** How many definitions are there for the word *wind*? ____

**4.** How many of the definitions did you already know? ____

**C.** Go online for more practice with using the dictionary.

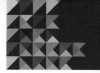

# WRITING

At the end of this unit, you will write a paragraph describing the steps of a process performed by either a person or a machine. This paragraph will include specific information from the readings and your own ideas.

## Writing Skill | Describing a process

When you write about a **process**, you describe how to do something step-by-step. First, you write a topic sentence that states what the process is. Then you explain each step clearly. Use **time order** words to help guide your reader. Time order words usually come at the beginning of a sentence and are followed by a comma. Note that *then* is not followed by a comma.

**Tip** for Success

Use several different time order words in your writing. This will help make your writing more interesting to the reader.

| first | next | then | later | after that | finally |
|-------|------|------|-------|------------|---------|

**First,** turn on your computer.
**Then** go to our website.

Use these time order words to link two steps in a process.

| after | as soon as | before | when | while |
|-------|------------|--------|------|-------|

**Before** you download the program, read the directions.
**While** the program is downloading, you can check your email.

**A.** **WRITING MODEL**  Read the model instructions for digital dining. Circle the time order words.

Digital dining is an easy way to order food. First, view the menu on your tabletop monitor. Then insert your credit card. Next, use the touch screen to enter your order. When you're ready, push the button to send your order. While you wait for your food, you can take photos and send them to your friends. Finally, use the monitor to pay your bill with a credit card. You see, it's easy to use digital dining!

**B.** Read the steps about how to use an ATM (automated teller machine). Then write the steps in the flow chart on page 140 to show the correct order.

Using an ATM

a. Press "withdraw."

b. Insert your ATM card.

c. Push "done."

d. Read the choices.

e. Remove the money from the slot.

f. Enter your PIN (personal identification number).

g. Enter the amount of money.

h. Take your receipt and your card.

**Process:** How to use an ATM

**Start**

**Finish**

**C.** Write the process from Activity B in a paragraph, using time order words. You may combine two steps into one sentence.

**D.** Think of a process that describes something that you know how to make, fix, or use. Then write notes for the steps in the flow chart. Add more boxes if you need to.

**Process:** _____

**Start**

**Finish**

**E.** Show your flow chart to a partner and explain the steps. Answer any questions about the process. Do you need to add additional steps or information? Add notes to your chart.

**F.** What are some things that sometimes go wrong in your process? What are some extra tips you can include? Complete the sentences on page 141 to give additional information about the process.

1. When you _____, be sure that you

   _____ .

2. Be careful when you _____ because sometimes

   _____ .

3. Don't forget to _____ . You will

   _____ if you don't _____ .

**G.** Use your flow chart and one or two sentences from activity F to write a paragraph describing a process. Make sure to use time order words.

 **H.** Go online for more practice with describing a process.

## Grammar   Infinitives of purpose

An **infinitive** is *to* + the base form of a verb. We sometimes use infinitives to show the purpose of an action. We call these **infinitives of purpose**. An infinitive of purpose is usually separated from the main verb in a sentence. Infinitives of purpose can be used with most action verbs.

**Follow** these steps **to use** an ATM.
   main verb    infinitive
               of purpose

**Push** the button **to send** your order.
main verb    infinitive
            of purpose

The manager **lowered** prices **to increase** sales.
            main verb    infinitive
                        of purpose

Sometimes an infinitive of purpose comes before the main verb.

**To use** an ATM, **follow** these steps.
infinitive       main verb
of purpose

Not all infinitives are infinitives of purpose. An infinitive of purpose has the same meaning as *in order to*. If you insert the phrase *in order to*, it will help you figure out if an infinitive is one that shows purpose.

Infinitive of purpose:

> He called me **to apologize.**
> He called me **in order to** apologize. (same meaning)

Not an infinitive of purpose:

> He called me and said that he wanted **to apologize.**
> He called me and said that he wanted **in order to apologize.** (not the same meaning and incorrect)

**A.** Circle each infinitive of purpose in the paragraph. Remember, not every infinitive shows purpose.

Creating your own online blog is a good way to connect with people who share your interests. I started a blog last year to share my experience as an international exchange student in Miami, Florida. It was very easy to do, and it allowed me to practice my writing skills and be in touch with other students. Here's how you do it. First, go online to find free blog websites. There are many available, but you should look for one that is easy to use. Start by looking at some sample blogs to get ideas for your own blog. Then get started! The site will tell you what to do for each step of the set-up process. After you have set up your blog, you can write your first post. Use photos to add visual interest to your page. Having a blog is a fun experience because you get comments from people who read it. It's also a great way to practice your writing skills and to think creatively.

**B.** Answer these questions using infinitives of purpose.

1. Why do you use the Internet?

   I use the internet (to get) information
   I use the internet (in order to get) informa

2. What is another kind of technology that you use? Why do you use it?

   I use my cell phone (to stay in contact) with my f

3. Why do companies use voice-automated telephone systems?

   Companies use voice-automated systems (to help
   customers faster

4. Why are you studying English?

*I am studying English (to improve) my communication.*

 **C.** Go online for more practice with infinitives of purpose.

**D.** Go online for the grammar expansion.

---

**Unit Assignment** | **Write a paragraph describing a process**

 In this assignment, you will write a paragraph describing a process done by either a person or a machine. As you prepare your paragraph, think about the Unit Question, "Do you prefer to get help from a person or a machine?" Use information from Reading 1, Reading 2, the unit video, and your work in this unit to support your paragraph. Refer to the Self-Assessment checklist on page 144.

 Go to the Online Writing Tutor for a writing model and alternate Unit Assignments.

## PLAN AND WRITE

**A.** **BRAINSTORM** Use the chart to brainstorm ideas for a topic. Then share your ideas with a partner. Decide which topics are the most interesting.

| Self-service technology and machines | Things I can make by myself | Things I can repair by myself |
| --- | --- | --- |
|  |  |  |
|  |  |  |
|  |  |  |

**Critical Thinking** Tip

In Activity B you **identify** the steps in a process. To describe a process, you have to break the process down into separate steps. **Identifying** the steps or parts of a process helps you to understand it better.

**B.** **PLAN** Complete the activities.

1. Look at your chart in Activity A and select a topic for your paragraph.

2. Think about how you will explain the steps of the process. Make a flow chart of the steps in order. Then make a list of time order words you can use to connect the steps of your process.

**C.** **WRITE** Use your **PLAN** notes to write your paragraph. Go to *iQ Online* to use the Online Writing Tutor.

1. Write a topic sentence for your paragraph. Then use your notes from Activity B to write your paragraph. Use time order words from the Writing Skill on page 139. Use infinitives of purpose where you can. Include sentences with additional tips and information about what can go wrong.

2. Look at the Self-Assessment checklist to guide your writing.

## REVISE AND EDIT

**A.** **PEER REVIEW** Read a partner's paragraph. Then go online and use the Peer Review worksheet. Discuss the review with your partner.

**B.** **REWRITE** Based on your partner's review, revise and rewrite your paragraph.

**C.** **EDIT** Complete the Self-Assessment checklist as you prepare to write the final draft of your paragraph. Be prepared to hand in your work or discuss it in class.

| SELF-ASSESSMENT | | |
|:---:|:---:|---|
| Yes | No | |
| ☐ | ☐ | Do you describe the process clearly using time order words? |
| ☐ | ☐ | Does your paragraph include infinitives of purpose? |
| ☐ | ☐ | Is each word spelled correctly? Check a dictionary if you are not sure. |
| ☐ | ☐ | Does the paragraph include vocabulary from the unit? |
| ☐ | ☐ | Did you check the paragraph for punctuation, spelling, and grammar? |

**D.** **REFLECT** Go to the Online Discussion Board to discuss these questions.

1. What is something new you learned in this unit?

2. Look back at the Unit Question—Do you prefer to get help from a person or a machine? Is your answer different now than when you started the unit? If yes, how is it different? Why?

# TRACK YOUR SUCCESS

**Circle the words and phrases you have learned in this unit.**

**Nouns**
access 🔑 AWL
benefit 🔑 AWL
connection 🔑
error 🔑 AWL

**Verbs**
assist 🔑 AWL
blame 🔑
decrease 🔑
estimate 🔑 AWL
install 🔑

interact AWL
provide 🔑
scan
transfer 🔑 AWL

**Adjectives**
frustrated
furious
stressed 🔑 AWL
unique 🔑 AWL

**Adverbs**
automatically 🔑 AWL
eventually 🔑 AWL

**Phrases**
on hold

🔑 Oxford 3000™ words
AWL Academic Word List

**Check (✓) the skills you learned. If you need more work on a skill, refer to the page(s) in parentheses.**

| | |
|---|---|
| **READING** ☐ | I can identify the author's purpose. (p. 131) |
| **VOCABULARY** ☐ | I can use the dictionary to identify the correct meanings of words. (p. 137) |
| **WRITING** ☐ | I can describe a step-by-step process. (p. 139) |
| **GRAMMAR** ☐ | I can use infinitives of purpose correctly. (pp. 141–142) |
| **UNIT OBJECTIVE** ▶▶▶▶ ☐ | I can gather information and ideas to write a paragraph describing the steps of a process. |

UNIT **7**

READING ▶ identifying fact and opinion
VOCABULARY ▶ phrasal verbs
WRITING ▶ using sentence variety
GRAMMAR ▶ simple past and past continuous

Environmental Studies

**UNIT QUESTION**

# Is it better to save what you have or buy new things?

**A** Discuss these questions with your classmates.

1. What are some things that people choose to have repaired when they are broken?

2. What is the oldest piece of clothing that you still wear? How old is it? Why do you still have it?

3. Look at the photo. Do you buy things when they go on sale?

 **B** Listen to *The Q Classroom* online. Then answer these questions.

1. Marcus says that old things become outdated. What does he mean?

2. Una says that that buying new things is good for the economy. What does she mean? Do you agree?

iQ ONLINE **C** Go to the Online Discussion Board to discuss the Unit Question with your classmates.

147

**D** Look at the quiz below. Answer the questions about garbage.

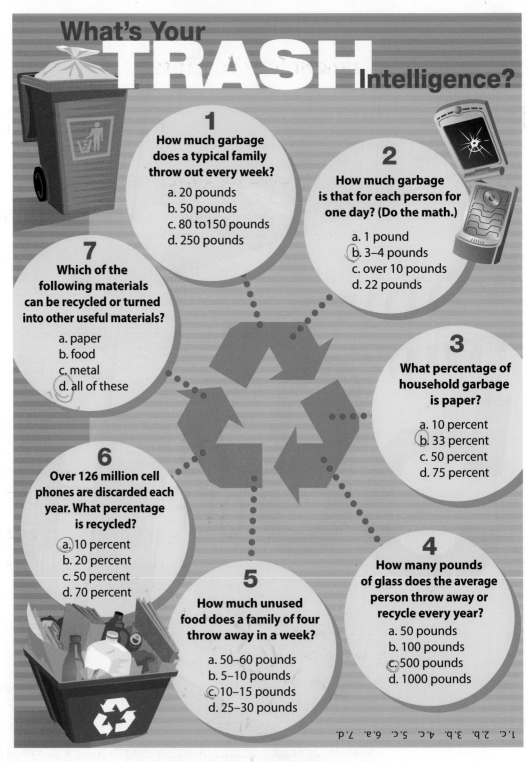

## What's Your TRASH Intelligence?

**1** How much garbage does a typical family throw out every week?

a. 20 pounds
b. 50 pounds
c. 80 to150 pounds
d. 250 pounds

**2** How much garbage is that for each person for one day? (Do the math.)

a. 1 pound
b. 3–4 pounds
c. over 10 pounds
d. 22 pounds

**3** What percentage of household garbage is paper?

a. 10 percent
b. 33 percent
c. 50 percent
d. 75 percent

**4** How many pounds of glass does the average person throw away or recycle every year?

a. 50 pounds
b. 100 pounds
c. 500 pounds
d. 1000 pounds

**5** How much unused food does a family of four throw away in a week?

a. 50–60 pounds
b. 5–10 pounds
c. 10–15 pounds
d. 25–30 pounds

**6** Over 126 million cell phones are discarded each year. What percentage is recycled?

a. 10 percent
b. 20 percent
c. 50 percent
d. 70 percent

**7** Which of the following materials can be recycled or turned into other useful materials?

a. paper
b. food
c. metal
d. all of these

1.c 2.b 3.b 4.c 5.c 6.a 7.d.

**E** Discuss your answers with a partner. Then look at the answers at the bottom of the quiz. How many did you get correct? Did any answers surprise you?

## READING 1 | Think Before You Toss

UNIT OBJECTIVE

You are going to read a magazine article about why we should keep things instead of throwing them away. Use the article to gather information and ideas for your Unit Assignment.

### PREVIEW THE READING

**Vocabulary Skill Review**

In Unit 6, you learned to use the dictionary to find the definition of words with more than one meaning. Using a dictionary, find two other meanings of the word *feature*.

**A.** **VOCABULARY** Here are some words from Reading 1. Read their definitions. Then complete each sentence.

> **attitude** (*noun*) 🔑 the way you think, feel, or behave
>
> **consequences** (*noun*) 🔑 things that follow as a result or effect of something else
>
> **consumer** (*noun*) 🔑 a person who buys things or uses services
>
> **disposable** (*adjective*) something you can throw away
>
> **factor** (*noun*) 🔑 one of the things that influences a decision or situation
>
> **feature** (*noun*) 🔑 an important or noticeable part of something
>
> **habit** (*noun*) 🔑 something that somebody does very often
>
> **persuade** (*verb*) 🔑 to cause somebody to do something by giving him or her good reason
>
> **possession** (*noun*) 🔑 something that you have or own

🔑 Oxford 3000™ words

1. Polluting the environment has serious _consequences_ for our society. For example, scientists say that air pollution can result in many health problems.

(consumer verb)

2. Miguelina's favorite _possession_ is the gold necklace her grandmother gave her. (possess) (verb)

3. Eating junk food is a bad _habit_. It's very unhealthy!

4. There are fewer people shopping in the mall this year than there were last year. The average _consumer_ is spending less than last year.

5. My brother worked hard to _persuade_ me to recycle more of my trash. I thought it would be too much trouble, but I changed my mind.

6. My printer has a new _feature_ I really like. It can scan photos and print them.

7. Sandra has a very positive _attitude_. She always has a cheerful outlook.

8. I can't decide which new car to buy, but the main _factor_ in my decision will be the price.

9. For the meal, we used _disposable_ glasses and plates. We didn't want to wash dishes after the meal, so we threw them away.

**B.** Go online for more practice with the vocabulary.

**C.** **PREVIEW** This article discusses some of the reasons we have too much trash and suggests some possible solutions. In the article, the author uses the term *throwaway society*. What do you think *throwaway society* means?

☐ It's a society that recycles a lot.

☐ It's a society that throws away a lot.

☐ It's a society that isn't important.

**D.** **QUICK WRITE** Write your responses to the questions below before you read the article. Be sure to use this section for your Unit Assignment.

1. If something you own is broken, do you usually fix it or do you usually buy something new?

2. What problems do you see with all of the trash that people throw away each year?

# WORK WITH THE READING

**A.** Read the article and gather information about saving what you have or buying new things.

# Think Before You Toss

*"Why don't you just take them to the shoe repairman? He'll put new soles[1] on, shine them up, and they'll be good for many more years," my grandfather suggested. I was complaining that my favorite shoes were falling apart after only six months.*

*"Grandpa, that shoe repairman went out of business years ago. No one repairs shoes anymore. And really, I don't mind. I'd rather buy a new pair of shoes, even if they don't last[2] that long."*

*"Nothing's built to last anymore," he sighed.*

1   Perhaps Grandpa has a point[3]. In our modern world, when something wears out, we throw it away and buy a replacement. If a shirt is torn or a coffee machine breaks, you throw it away. The problem is that countries around the world have growing mountains of trash because people are throwing out more trash than ever before. For example, in the United States, the amount of trash per person more than doubled from 1960 to 2014.

2   How did we become a throwaway society? First of all, it is now easier to replace an item than to spend time and money to repair it. Thanks to modern manufacturing and technology, companies are able to produce items quickly and inexpensively. Products are plentiful and prices are low, so we would rather buy something new than repair it. Even if we did want to repair something, many items— from toasters to TVs—are almost impossible to repair. These products contain many tiny, complicated parts. Some even contain small computer chips. It's easier to throw these items away and buy new ones than to fix them.

3   Another contributing **factor** is our love of **disposable** products. As busy people, we are always looking for ways to save time and make our lives easier. Why should we use cloth kitchen towels? It is easier to use a paper towel once and toss it out. Companies manufacture thousands of different kinds of disposable items: paper plates, plastic cups, cameras, and razors for

---

[1] **soles:** the part of the shoe that covers the bottom
[2] **last:** to remain in good condition

[3] **have a point:** to have an important comment in a discussion

shaving, to name a few. Because these products aren't designed to last, companies know that **consumers** will have to replace them, buying them over and over again. "What's wrong with that?" you ask. The problem is that disposable products are contributing to our trash problem.

4   Our appetite for new products also contributes to the problem. We are addicted to[4] buying new things. As consumers, we want the latest clothes, the best TVs, and cell phones with the newest **features**. Companies tell us to buy, buy, and buy. Advertisements **persuade** us that newer is better and that we will be happier with the latest products. The result is that we throw away useful **possessions** to make room for new ones. In the U.S., when consumers get rid of electronics, 70 percent of them go to a dump. Only about 30 percent of electronics are recycled.

5   All around the world, we can see the **consequences** of this throwaway lifestyle. Dumpsites are mountains of garbage that just keep getting bigger. To decrease the amount of trash and to protect the environment, more governments are requiring people to recycle materials such as paper, plastic, and glass. However, only a small portion of what can be recycled is actually recycled. For example, in the United Kingdom, only 43 percent of household trash is actually

recycled. Even though recycling helps, it's not enough to solve our problem of too much trash.

6   Maybe there is another solution. First, we need to repair our possessions instead of throwing them away. As consumers, we should think about how to fix something to make it last. Furthermore, we need to rethink our **attitudes** about spending. Do we really need the latest clothing styles when our closets are full of clothes? Repairing our possessions and changing our spending **habits** may be the best way to reduce the amount of trash and take care of our environment.

| What can you do to waste less? | |
| --- | --- |
| Think before you buy. | Sell it. |
| Fix it or get it repaired. | Give it away. |
| Recycle it. | |

---

[4] **addicted to:** unable to stop

**B. Answer these questions. Underline the sentences in the reading where you found the answers.**

1. What is the grandfather's opinion about products made today?

   *Nothing build to last anymore.*

2. Why are there "growing mountains of trash" in various parts of the world?

   _____

3. The author says that we are a "throwaway society." What does that mean?

   *repair*

   *We do not Fixed.*
   *Everybody dosen't.*

4. What examples does the author give of disposable items?

_paper plate, paper cup._

5. Why do consumers like disposable products?

_save time, they are convenient._

6. Why do companies like disposable products?

_people throw away and buy more._

7. What is the result of our addiction to buying new things?

_creates garbage._

8. The author gives her opinion in the last paragraph. What is it?

_people should repair instead of throw away._

**C. Answer these questions.**

1. What examples does the author give of products that we usually don't repair? _Toaster and TV_

2. Why are companies able to make products more quickly and at lower cost? _modern manufacturing_

3. Why are some things difficult to repair? _Tiny complicated parts._

4. What are four reasons we throw things away? _old, broken, cheaper to replace, disposable._

5. Why do consumers often get rid of useful possessions? _People want the new version._

6. What do these numbers refer to in the article?
   a. 1960–2012: _the amount trash doubled_
   b. 70 percent, 30 percent: _go to the dump, 30% are recycled_
   c. 43 percent: _is actually recycled in U.K._

**D.** Look back at Reading 1 and find three questions. Write them below. Does the author already know the answers? Why does she ask them? Discuss your answer with a partner.

_____

_____

_____

**E. Match the causes with the effects.**

_c_ 1. People are throwing more things away.

_e_ 2. People think that new things are better.

_b_ 3. Prices are low.

_a_ 4. Products are not designed to last for a long time

_d_ 5. Some products have complicated parts.

a. People need to replace disposable products.

b. People would rather buy a new item than repair an old item.

c. There are large quantities of trash around the world.

d. They are difficult to repair.

e. Useful possessions are thrown away.

iQ ONLINE **F. Go online to read *Sell Your Stuff Online* and check your comprehension.**

## WRITE WHAT YOU THINK

**A. Discuss these questions in a group.**

1. What items (clothing, electronics, sports equipment) have you recently thrown away? Could the items have been repaired? Why or why not? Did you replace them with something new?

2. Think of something that is still useful, but that you no longer want. What can you do with that item instead of throwing it away?

3. Do you think recycling is important? What kind of things do you recycle?

**B. Choose one of the questions and write a multiple sentence response. Look back at your Quick Write on page 150 as you think about what you learned.**

Question: _____

My Response: _____

_____

_____

_____

A **fact** is something that people generally agree is true. Facts are sometimes supported by statistics or other numbers.

> Water freezes at 0° Celsius.
> Paper is one of the easiest materials to recycle.
> In the United States, 18 percent of old TVs are recycled.

*True* [handwritten]

An **opinion** is what a person thinks about something. Another person may not agree.

> English is an easy language to learn.
> Consumers are more interested in a product's price than in its quality.
> Advertising has a bad influence on our spending habits.

When reading, it's helpful to understand the difference between facts and opinions. Some words that can indicate an opinion are: *(not) think*, *(not) believe*, *(not) feel*, and *in my opinion*.

> I **don't think** English is an easy language to learn.
> The author **believes** advertising has a bad influence on our spending habits.

**A.** Read these sentences from Reading 1. Write *F* (fact) or *O* (opinion). Then compare your answers with a partner.

_F_ 1. It is now easier to replace an item than to repair it.

_F_ 2. Many materials such as paper, plastic, and glass can be recycled, but only a small percentage of these are actually recycled.

_O_ 3. Perhaps recycling is not the answer.

_O_ 4. We should think about repairing something before we toss it in the trash.

_O_ 5. We are all responsible for taking care of our environment.

_F_ 6. People are throwing away twice as much trash as they did 40 years ago.

**B.** Write a sentence with an opinion and a fact about each topic. For your opinion sentences, use *(not) think*, *(not) believe*, *(not) feel*, or *in my opinion*.

1. color

   Fact: _Colors can affect how people feel._

   Opinion: _I think pink is a beautiful color._

2. cell phones

Fact: _Cell phones help people stay in touch with family and friends._

Opinion: _Cell phones are necesary. I think we sho spend less time on our phones._

3. recycling plastic, paper, and glass

Fact: _The city of lake worth recycles paper._

Opinion: _Recycling is good for the environment._

4. shopping online

Fact: _Shopping online saves time_

Opinion: _Amazon is the best website._

 **C. Go online** for more practice with identifying fact and opinion.

## READING 2 | In Praise of the Throwaway Society

UNIT OBJECTIVE ▶▶▶ You are going to read a blog post. In the blog, a man gives his opinion about the throwaway society. Use the blog post to gather information and ideas for your Unit Assignment.

## PREVIEW THE READING

**A. VOCABULARY** Here are some words from Reading 2. Read the sentences. Then match each <u>underlined</u> word with its definition on page 157.

1. I've never heard the <u>term</u> *throwaway society*. What does it mean?

2. Sun Joon is a very <u>materialistic</u> person. She seems more interested in shopping than making friends.

3. Paul's old jacket is <u>patched</u> on the elbows where it used to be ripped.

4. If there's a <u>significant</u> amount of snow, the schools will close.

5. Do you think that life forms <u>exist</u> in outer space?

6. New flowers in the garden are a <u>sign</u> that spring is here.

7. My old cell phone works pretty well, but I really want to get a new <u>model</u>.

8. After the soccer game, Khalid put on a <u>fresh</u> shirt and put his dirty one in the wash.

Oxford 3000™ words

9. Kevin and Tanya made a <u>budget</u> for March, but they spent more than they had planned.

10. Yuki thought that the new phone would cost $50, but the <u>actual</u> cost was higher.

a. _budget_ (*noun*) a plan of how much money you will have and how you will spend it

b. _exist_ (*verb*) to be real; to live

c. _fresh_ (*adjective*) clean or new

d. _materialistic_ (*adjective*) believing that money and possessions are the most important things in life

e. _model_ (*noun*) a certain style of an item that a company makes

f. _patched_ (*adjective*) covered with cloth to repair a hole

g. _sign_ (*noun*) something that shows that something exists, is happening, or may happen in the future

h. _significant_ (*adjective*) important or large enough to be noticed

i. _therm_ (*noun*) a word or group of words

j. _actual_ (*adjective*) that really happened; real

**B.** Go online for more practice with the vocabulary.

iQ ONLINE

**C.** **PREVIEW** The author of the blog has an opinion that is different from the opinion given in Reading 1. What do you think he will say about a throwaway society?

☐ In a throwaway society, no one should recycle.

☐ A throwaway society shows that people are doing well.

☒ Wealthy people don't need to throw anything away.

**D.** **QUICK WRITE** Some people feel that it is foolish to repair old things. They believe that we should just buy new things. What are some advantages of buying new things? Write a few sentences. Be sure to use this section for your Unit Assignment.

**Tip** for Success

Remember that when writing online, people often use informal language. For example, they may use informal words and phrases. (stuff = things) They may also begin sentences with *But* or *And*.

# WORK WITH THE READING

⟐ **A.** Read the blog post and gather information about saving what you have or buying new things.

---

## Mad Anthony

Opinions and thoughts on politics, technology, life, and other stuff

**Home**          **Log in**

---

### In Praise of the Throwaway Society

**About**

JANUARY 26, 2015                                      COMMENTS 16

**Links**

**Archives**

1   Yesterday, I heard someone use the phrase *throwaway society*, which got me thinking. Usually, the **term** *throwaway society* is used as a way of saying that we are too **materialistic**. It means that too much of our stuff today is of poor quality instead of being built to last.

January

February

2   I see things the opposite way. The fact that we live in a throwaway society isn't a **sign** that things are worse than they used to be. It is a sign that things are better than they have ever been. True, we don't repair things as much as we used to. But that's because we don't have to and don't want to, not because we can't. And it's better that way.

March

April

May

June

3   I say this because being able to replace instead of repair shows that people are wealthy. What would you rather have: an old repaired laptop or the latest **model**? A pair of socks with the hole **patched** or a **fresh** pair? Some people think that products today are less dependable than they used to be. But most people would rather have something with a newer design, and they vote with their wallets[1].

July

August

September

October

November

4   I think there are three reasons for this. First, lower prices. Today, because of technology, it costs less to make items, so they sell for less. When the price difference is small or when it costs more to fix an item than to replace it, consumers naturally decide to pick up a new one. Second, increased wealth. People have more money than they did in the past, and because of lower prices, they can afford more things. A hundred years ago, most people had one or two sets of clothes. Those clothes were valuable and expensive and formed a **significant** part of their **budget**. Now, you can get a nice sweater for a few dollars. It isn't expensive at all. When that sweater gets a hole in it, you toss it and buy a new one because you can afford to.

December

5   Third, increased features. Thanks to advances in technology, products are getting better all the time, especially electronics. There is a good chance that the latest model includes some cool features that didn't **exist** when your old one

---

[1] **vote with their wallets:** show their opinion by buying what they want

---

was made. Now, you can get a high-definition[2] digital camera that is small enough to fit in your hand. You can get cell phones that have everything from email to video to GPS[3]. In fact, I hardly ever use my phone for an **actual** phone call anymore because it can do so many other wonderful things. You see, the benefit of increased features is another reason to buy something new. So throw something out today! The throwaway society shows us how good things are.

**About Me**

Who am I? I am a 28-year-old living in Baltimore, Maryland, in the United States. I grew up in New Jersey, but I went to college in Baltimore and stayed. Now I work at that college in a tech support position. My hobbies include blogging, fooling around[4] with computers, sleeping, selling stuff online, and yelling at the TV.

---

[2] **high definition:** very good quality
[3] **GPS (global positioning system):** digital tool that can tell you your location

[4] **fooling around:** not taking something seriously; playing or experimenting with something

**B. Read the statements. Are they true or false according to the author of Reading 2? Write *T* (true) and *F* (false).**

_T_ 1. Most people think that *throwaway society* means we are too materialistic.

_F_ 2. The author thinks it is too bad that we don't repair things as much as we used to.

_F_ 3. People vote with their wallets by not buying new things.

_F_ 4. Because of technology, the cost of new items has gone up.

_T_ 5. Today more people can easily afford to buy new clothes.

_F_ 6. New products have too many features to be useful.

_F_ 7. Our throwaway society is going to cause problems in the future.

**C. Circle the answer that best completes each statement. Then underline the place in the reading where you found the answer.**

1. According to Mad Anthony, the throwaway society is a sign that …
   a. society has become too materialistic.
   b. things are worse than they used to be.
   c. things are better than they have ever been.

2. Mad Anthony says that …
   a. people would rather have something new.
   b. we can't repair things as easily as before.
   c. replacing instead of repairing is a sign of a weak society.

3. People buy clothing instead of repairing it because ...

    a. clothing today is very valuable.

    (b.) it doesn't cost much to buy new clothes.

    c. clothing forms a significant part of their budget.

4. The author thinks that one reason people buy new things is ...

    (a.) their old model doesn't have the latest features.

    b. cell phones are no longer useful for making actual phone calls.

    c. too many features make new models complicated.

5. The author of this reading thinks that people should ...

    a. fix items rather than replace things.

    b. take pictures with their cell phones.

    (c.) throw things away when they're old.

**D.** **Complete each sentence with information from Reading 2. Then look at Reading 2 to check your answers.**

1. Today, because of technology, it costs ___less___ to make items, so products sell for ___less___.

2. When the price difference is ___small___ or when it costs ___more___ to fix an item than to ___replace___ it, consumers naturally decide to pick up a new one.

3. People have ___more___ money than they did in the past, and because of ___lower___ prices, people can ___afford___ more things.

4. Thanks to advances in technology, products are getting ___better___ all the time.

5. The ___benefit___ of increased features is another ___reason___ to buy something new.

# WRITE WHAT YOU THINK

**A.** **Discuss these questions in a group. Look back at your Quick Write on page 157 as you think about what you learned.**

1. Do you think it is better to save and wear old clothing or to buy new, trendy clothes? Why?

2. Mad Anthony gives reasons to support his opinion that the throwaway society is a good thing. Do you think these are good reasons? Why or why not?

**B.** Go online to watch the video about a man who recycles items found in the trash. Then check your comprehension.

VIDEO VOCABULARY

**dumpster** *(n.)* large outdoor container for trash

**gather up** *(phr. v.)* to collect; pick up

**notion** *(n.)* idea

**refuse** *(n.)* trash or things thrown away

Critical Thinking (Tip)

Question 2 asks you to **devise**, or think of, a new way to use an unwanted item. **Devising** means that you have to put information and ideas together in a new way.

**C.** Think about the unit video, Reading 1, and Reading 2 as you discuss these questions. Then choose one question and write a response.

1. What are some of the advantages of buying new things instead of fixing old things? Give examples.

2. Some people make new things from old items. For example, some artists make jewelry from old computer parts. What are some new ways you can use something you normally throw away?

## Vocabulary Skill    Phrasal verbs

A **phrasal verb** is a *verb* + a *particle*. Some examples of particles are *in, out, up, over, by, down,* and *away*. When a particle is added to a verb, it often creates a new meaning.

I want to **watch** the game on TV tonight.    (watch = look at)
**Watch out** for ice on the stairs!    (watch out = be careful)

Many phrasal verbs have more than one meaning.

He **picked up** the book and started to read.    (lifted)
Abdullah **picked up** his friend in his new red car.    (gave a ride to)
The wind **picked up** in the afternoon.    (increased)

Some phrasal verbs are **separable**. They can be separated by objects.

He **picked up** the book.        Yolanda **threw away** her old shoes.
He **picked** the book **up**.        Yolanda **threw** her old shoes **away**.

Some phrasal verbs are **inseparable**. They cannot be separated by an object.

✓ Ollie **fell down** the stairs.    ✓ Eva **stopped by** my house yesterday.
✗ Ollie **fell** the stairs **down**.    ✗ Eva **stopped** my house **by** yesterday.

**A. Read the sentences. Then circle the answer that best matches the meaning of each bold phrasal verb.**

1. I **wore out** my favorite jeans, so I bought a new pair.
   a. repaired    (b.) used too much

2. Don't **throw out** the newspaper. I want to read the sports page.
   (a.) put in the trash    b. put outside

3. It's raining, so I'm going to **put on** my raincoat.
   a. wash    (b.) wear

4. You shouldn't **throw away** plastic bottles. You should recycle them.
   a. reuse    (b.) put in the trash

5. The shoes at that store are very cheap, but they are not good quality, so they **fall apart** easily.
   a. look nice    (b.) break into pieces

**B. Rewrite the sentences putting the object between the verb and the particle.**

1. We picked up the children from school.

   _We picked the children up from school._

2. Please throw away your trash. Don't leave it in the park.

   _____

3. Put on your hat. It's very cold outside!

   _____

4. I'm going to throw out my old watch and buy a new one.

   _____

5. I walk a lot, so I wear out my shoes quickly.

   _____

**iQ** ONLINE    **C. Go online for more practice with phrasal verbs.**

At the end of this unit, you will write an opinion paragraph. This paragraph will include specific information from the readings and your own ideas.

---

## Writing Skill   Using sentence variety

When you write, it's important to use different types of sentences. Using different types of sentences makes your writing more interesting to read. Here are some ways to improve your **sentence variety**.

- Use long and short sentences.
- If you have too many short sentences, combine two sentences into one with a coordinating conjunction (*and*, *but*, or *so*).
- Use questions and imperatives.

**Look at these examples from Reading 1.**

> Perhaps Grandpa has a point. In our modern world, when something wears out, we throw it away and buy a replacement.

> Products are plentiful and prices are low, so we would rather buy something new than repair it.

> Why should we use cloth kitchen towels? It is easier to use a paper towel once and toss it out.

**A.** **WRITING MODEL**   Read the model paragraph. Then do tasks 1–4 below. Compare your answers with a partner.

Do you prefer to fix what you have or buy new things? I usually fix the things I have, but I always buy new shoes. I love buying shoes. I already have lots of shoes in different styles and colors, but I always find a new pair that I want to buy. Sometimes after class, I meet my friend Sue. We have coffee, and then we go shopping for shoes at the new shopping center downtown. It's a nice way to spend the afternoon. Are your shoes old and worn out? Don't fix them. Buy a new pair. It's fun!

1. Circle the short sentences in the paragraph.

2. Underline the long sentences in the paragraph.

3. Put a check (✓) next to the questions.

4. Put a star next to the imperatives.

**B.** Take the two short sentences and make them one long sentence. Use *and*, *but*, or *so*.

1. I try to recycle things, Other people in my family usually just throw things away. *but* .

   _____

2. It was raining all day, My clothes got wet. *, so* .

   _____

3. I wasn't wearing a raincoat, I might catch a cold. *, so* ,

   _____

4. Vladimir likes to buy new clothes, His sister Maria likes to buy new clothes, too. *and*

   _____

5. I wish vacation were longer. School starts on Monday. *, but*

   _____

**C.** WRITING MODEL Rewrite the model paragraph below and use more sentence variety. You can combine sentences, change sentences, and add more sentences to the paragraph.

Earlier this year, some students noticed that recycling was difficult at our school. There were no containers to collect paper for recycling. People just threw paper away. Also, many students drink bottled water. They throw bottles in the trash without thinking. Student organizers made posters about recycling. They put containers for recycling paper in every classroom and office. In one month, there was a significant increase in the amount of paper in the containers. There were also more bottles in the containers. The organizers are very happy with the results. They hope people's habits continue to change. They hope attitudes change, too.

**D.** Write an outline for a paragraph giving your opinion on this statement: *Everyone should be required to recycle.* Write some notes to help you state your opinion in a topic sentence, give reasons to support your opinion, and form a concluding sentence.

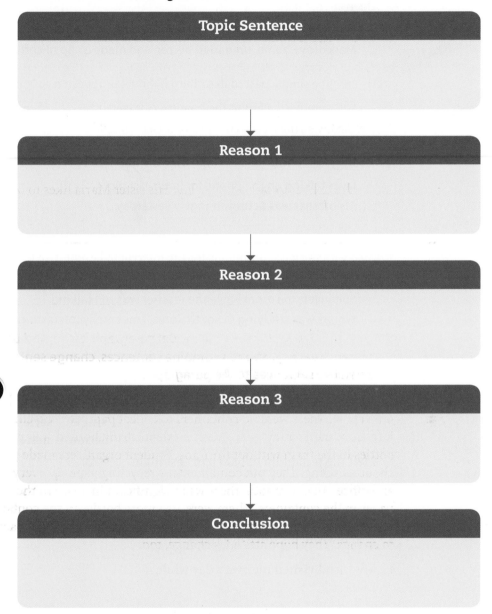

**Topic Sentence**

**Reason 1**

**Reason 2**

**Reason 3**

**Conclusion**

**Writing Tip**

In an opinion paragraph, support your opinion with reasons, details, and examples. Your concluding sentence should restate your opinion. Review the phrases on page 91 for writing an opinion paragraph. *I think that, I believe that,* or *I feel that* are useful for expressing opinions.

**E.** Write a paragraph based on your notes from Activity D. Use complete sentences with a variety of sentence types. Include some useful expressions for writing an opinion paragraph.

**F.** Share your writing with a classmate. Did you use useful sentences for giving opinions? Did you use a variety of sentence types? Rewrite your paragraph based on the feedback from your classmate.

**iQ ONLINE** **G.** Go online for more practice with sentence variety.

## Grammar | Simple past and past continuous

Use the **simple past** to describe a single completed action or a series of completed actions in the past.

> I **bought** the new novel by my favorite author yesterday.
> Mark **drove** home, **unloaded** his car, and **made** a cup of coffee.

Also use the simple past to describe a habitual or repeated action in the past.

> Last summer, I **went** to the park every weekend.
> I **sent** Leila three emails, but she never replied.

Use the **past continuous** to emphasize the duration of an action in the past.

> I **was talking** on the phone for hours last night.
> My brother **was acting** strangely yesterday.

If a past event was interrupted by another event or series of events, use *while* or *when* with the past continuous for the interrupted event. Use the simple past for the event or events that interrupted it.

> Sultan **left** the room <u>while</u> the teacher **was** still **talking**.
> <u>When</u> I **was studying** in South Korea, I **met** many interesting people.

**A.** Read the sentences. Check (✓) the function of the simple past (in bold) in the sentence.

|  | single action | series of actions | repeated action |
|---|:---:|:---:|:---:|
| 1. I **left** the restaurant at 6:00 p.m. last night. | ✓ | ☐ | ☐ |
| 2. When the president **came** into the room, everyone **stood** up and **clapped**. | ☐ | ✓ | ☐ |
| 3. Eric **rewrote** his story five times. | ☐ | ☐ | ✓ |
| 4. My friend **visited** me every day while I was sick. | ☐ | ☐ | ✓ |
| 5. Someone **stole** my bike last week. | ✓ | ☐ | ☐ |
| 6. Jessica **finished** her letter, **put** it in an envelope, and **took** it to the post office. | ☐ | ✓ | ☐ |

**B.** Read the sentences. Check (✓) the function of the past continuous (in bold) in the sentence.

| | duration | interrupted action |
|---|---|---|
| 1. Jim broke his leg while he **was playing** soccer. | ☐ | ☑ |
| 2. I **was watching** TV all weekend. | ☑ | ☐ |
| 3. When Natalia **was working** in the science lab, she discovered a mistake. | ☐ | ☑ |
| 4. You **were complaining** the whole time at the restaurant last night. | ☑ | ☐ |

**C.** Go online for more practice with the simple past and the past continuous.

**D.** Go online for the grammar expansion.

---

## Unit Assignment    Write an opinion paragraph

**UNIT OBJECTIVE** ▶▶▶▶

In this assignment, you will write an opinion paragraph. As you prepare your paragraph, think about the Unit Question, "Is it better to save what you have or buy new things?" Use information from Reading 1, Reading 2, the unit video, and your work in this unit to support your opinion. Refer to the Self-Assessment checklist on page 168.

Go to the Online Writing Tutor for a writing model and alternate Unit Assignments.

## PLAN AND WRITE

**A.** **BRAINSTORM** Brainstorm ideas about the Unit Question. Write as many ideas as you can.

**Tip for Success**

In a test situation, you need to quickly organize your ideas before you write your answer. An informal outline is a quick and easy way to plan your writing.

**B.** **PLAN** Make an informal outline to organize your ideas.

It's better to _____

Reason 1: _____

Reason 2: _____

Reason 3: _____

**C.** **WRITE** Use your **PLAN** notes to write your paragraph. Go to *iQ Online* to use the Online Writing Tutor.

1. Write your paragraph, using your notes from Activity B. Start with a clear topic sentence and include ideas that support your opinion. Finish with a strong concluding sentence. Try to use some useful expressions for giving opinions, some phrasal verbs, and the simple past or past continuous.

2. Look at the Self-Assessment checklist to guide your writing.

## REVISE AND EDIT

**A.** **PEER REVIEW** Read your partner's paragraph. Then go online and use the Peer Review worksheet. Discuss the review with your partner.

**B.** **REWRITE** Based on your partner's review, revise and rewrite your paragraph.

**C.** **EDIT** Complete the Self-Assessment checklist as you prepare to write the final draft of your paragraph. Be prepared to hand in your work or discuss it in class.

| SELF-ASSESSMENT | | |
|---|---|---|
| Yes | No | |
| ☐ | ☐ | Do you give a strong opinion and support it with facts? |
| ☐ | ☐ | Do you use a variety of sentence types to make your writing more interesting to read? |
| ☐ | ☐ | Do you use simple past and past continuous verbs correctly? |
| ☐ | ☐ | Circle any phrasal verbs you used in your paragraph. Do they express your ideas clearly? |
| ☐ | ☐ | Does the paragraph include vocabulary from the unit? |
| ☐ | ☐ | Did you check the paragraph for punctuation, spelling, and grammar? |

**D.** **REFLECT** Go to the Online Discussion Board to discuss these questions.

1. What is something new you learned in this unit?

2. Look back at the Unit Question—Is it better to save what you have or buy new things? Is your answer different now than when you started the unit? If yes, how is it different? Why?

# TRACK YOUR SUCCESS

**Circle the words and phrases you have learned in this unit.**

**Nouns**
attitude 🔑 AWL
budget 🔑
consequence 🔑 AWL
consumer 🔑 AWL
factor 🔑 AWL
feature 🔑 AWL
habit 🔑
model 🔑
possession 🔑
sign 🔑
term 🔑

**Verbs**
exist 🔑
persuade 🔑

**Phrasal Verbs**
fall apart
fall down
pick up
put on
stop by
throw away
throw out
watch out
wear out

**Adjectives**
actual 🔑
disposable AWL
fresh 🔑
materialistic
patched
significant 🔑 AWL

🔑 Oxford 3000™ words

AWL Academic Word List

**Check (✓) the skills you learned. If you need more work on a skill, refer to the page(s) in parentheses.**

| | |
|---|---|
| **READING** ☐ | I can identify facts and opinions. (p. 155) |
| **VOCABULARY** ☐ | I can use phrasal verbs. (p. 161) |
| **WRITING** ☐ | I can use sentence variety. (p. 163) |
| **GRAMMAR** ☐ | I can use the simple past and the past continuous. (p. 166) |
| **UNIT OBJECTIVE** ▶▶▶▶ ☐ | I can gather information and ideas to write an opinion paragraph. |

READING ▶ synthesizing information
VOCABULARY ▶ collocations
WRITING ▶ writing an explanatory paragraph
GRAMMAR ▶ adverbs of manner and degree

UNIT QUESTION

# How can we prevent diseases?

**A** Discuss these questions with your classmates.

1. When was the last time you were sick? How did you feel? How did you get sick?

2. What are some things you do to avoid getting sick?

3. Look at the photo. Who do you think the people are? What are they doing?

UNIT
OBJECTIVE 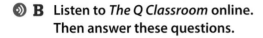 Read the articles. Gather information and ideas to
create an FAQ (Frequently Asked Questions) page that
begins with an explanatory paragraph about an illness.

**B** Listen to *The Q Classroom* online.
Then answer these questions.

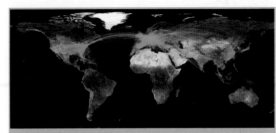

Disease can spread anywhere in 24 hours.

1. What six ways to prevent disease
did the speakers mention? Fill in
the chart below. Then for each one,
check (✓) how often you do it. When
you finish, discuss your chart with
your classmates.

| | Ways to prevent diseases | | | | |
|---|---|---|---|---|---|
| | | Always | Sometimes | Rarely | Never |
| a. | eat right | | | | |
| b. | Exercise. | | | | |
| c. | Wash Hands. | | | | |
| d. | Vaccination | | | | |
| e. | wade mask | | | | |
| f. | Stay Home | | | | |

2. Do you agree with Sophy and Felix that people should wear face masks or
stay home when they are sick? Why or why not?

**iQ ONLINE** **C** Go to the Online Discussion Board to discuss the Unit Question
with your classmates.

**D** Work with a partner. Match the name of each illness with the correct photo.

| | | |
|---|---|---|
| diabetes | malaria | influenza (flu) |
| asthma | skin cancer | tuberculosis (TB) |

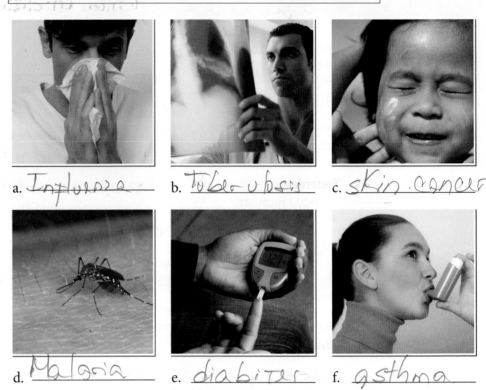

a. _Influenza_   b. _Tuberculosis_   c. _skin cancer_

d. _Malaria_   e. _diabites_   f. _asthma_

**E** Write the illness from Activity D next to the correct description.

1. _Skin canar_: Sun exposure is the leading cause of this disease. This disease causes cells to grow quickly.

2. _Malaria_: This is a serious disease that you can get from mosquito bites.

3. _tuberculosis_: This disease affects the lungs and spreads from person to person very easily.

4. _Asthma_: This condition causes difficulty in breathing. Using an inhaler (something to help people breathe more easily) can help.

5. _diabetes_: With this disease, the body cannot process sugar correctly.

6. _Influenza_: With this common illness, a person is sick for one to two weeks.

**F** Work with a partner. Discuss illnesses that spread from person to person.

# READING

## READING 1 | Flu FAQ (Frequently Asked Questions)

**UNIT OBJECTIVE** ▶▶▶▶ You are going to read a Web page from a health website. Use the Web page to gather information and ideas for your Unit Assignment.

### PREVIEW THE READING

**A. VOCABULARY** Here are some words from Reading 1. Read the sentences. Then write each <u>underlined</u> word next to the correct definition.

1. Yesterday <u>approximately</u> 50 students were home with the flu. I don't know the exact number.

2. You should <u>cover</u> your baby with extra blankets in the winter so he doesn't get cold.

3. I hope my cold doesn't <u>develop</u> into a bad cough. It's already worse than it was yesterday.

4. During the <u>epidemic</u>, every home in the town had at least one sick family member.

5. Colds are <u>extremely</u> common among school children during winter. Both of my children have colds right now.

6. If you have a cold and you sneeze on other people, you can <u>infect</u> them.

7. Your overall health is directly <u>related to</u> how well you eat and how often you exercise.

8. Pria had a <u>severe</u> pain in her back, so I took her to the hospital.

9. A sore throat is a common <u>symptom</u> of a cold.

10. A <u>virus</u> causes the common cold. It spreads from person to person quickly.

a. _related to_ (*adjective*) connected with something

b. _symptom_ (*noun*) something that shows that you have an illness

c. _virus_ (*noun*) a living thing that is too small to see but that makes you sick

d. _cover_ (*verb*) to put something on or in front of something else to protect it

_Infection (noun)_

e. _infect_ (*verb*) to give a disease to someone

_(sevior)_ f. _severe_ (*adjective*) very bad

_severely (adv)_

g. _extremely_ (adverb) very

h. _develop_ (verb) to grow slowly, increase, or change into something else

i. _approximately_ (adverb) about; not exactly

j. _epidemic_ (noun) a disease that many people in a place have at the same time

iQ ONLINE **B.** Go online for more practice with the vocabulary.

**C.** PREVIEW This online FAQ (Frequently Asked Questions) page is from a health website about the flu. FAQ pages state commonly asked questions about a topic, followed by the answers. Read the questions in the headings. Which ones can you answer without reading the answers?

**D.** QUICK WRITE Think about the last time you had a bad cold or the flu. Write your responses to the questions before you read the Web page. Be sure to use this section for your Unit Assignment.

1. What were your symptoms?

2. How long were you sick? Did you stay home from school or work?

3. What helped you feel better while you were sick?

## WORK WITH THE READING

**A.** Read the Web page and gather information about how we can prevent diseases.

# Flu FAQ (Frequently Asked Questions)

Flu season is coming! Are you prepared? Here are answers to your questions!

### What is the flu?

1    The flu, short for *influenza*, is a **virus** that passes easily from person to person. Every year, millions of people miss work and school because of the seasonal flu. Seasonal flu exists worldwide. Usually the flu season is in the winter months, but in warm climates, the flu occurs during the rainy season.

### What are the symptoms of the flu?

2    Flu **symptoms** include fever, cough, sore throat, body aches, headache, chills, and fatigue[1]. These symptoms usually show up quickly, **developing** within three to six hours of exposure to the virus. With the flu,

---

[1] **fatigue:** great tiredness

you may start the day feeling fine, only to end up feeling terrible a few hours later.

## What's the difference between the flu and a cold?

3 Both are respiratory[2] illnesses, but they are caused by different viruses. Although the symptoms can be similar, flu symptoms are more **severe** and include a high fever and body aches. Cold symptoms include a runny or stuffy[3] nose and a cough. You may have a slight fever with a cold, but in general, cold symptoms are milder and only last about seven days. The flu can last up to two weeks. It is much more likely to develop into a serious illness and require hospitalization.

## Who gets the flu?

4 The seasonal flu is very common all over the world. In the United States, 5 to 20 percent of the population gets the flu every year. After you have had the flu, you have immunity[4] to that virus. You will not get that particular virus again. However, new flu viruses appear every year. Even if you have the flu this year, you will not have immunity to next year's virus. Some people get the flu every year.

## Why is the flu dangerous?

5 The flu is especially dangerous for children aged 2 and under, adults over 65 years old, and people in poor health. These people may not be able to fight the virus and can become **extremely** sick. Every year in the U.S., there are **approximately** 36,000 deaths **related to** the seasonal flu.

## How does the flu spread?

6 Coughing or sneezing spreads flu viruses from person to person. A virus can live in a tiny drop of liquid from a cough for several hours, and it can live on a surface such as a table for up to 24 hours. A person can **infect** others before flu symptoms even develop and up to five days after becoming sick. You can pass the flu to someone else before you know you are sick.

## What's a flu epidemic?

7 A flu **epidemic** is when many people have the flu at the same time, and the number of infected people increases rapidly. Worldwide, annual flu epidemics result in about 3 to 5 million cases of severe illness, and about 250,000 to 500,000 deaths.

## How can I avoid getting the flu?

8 Many people get a flu vaccine[5] before the flu season starts. The U.S. Center for Disease Control and Prevention says that flu vaccines can prevent 70 percent to 90 percent of infections in healthy people under age 65. However, each year there are new, unknown viruses. Therefore, scientists must develop new vaccines each year. It can take 6 months to a year to develop these vaccines. For some viruses, there is no vaccine.

## What else can I do?

9 There are many things you can do to stay healthy and prevent the spread of the flu.

- Wash your hands often with soap and water or a liquid hand cleaner. Hand washing is the best way to prevent the spread of flu viruses.
- **Cover** your nose and mouth with a tissue when you cough or sneeze. Throw the tissue in the trash after you use it. If you don't have a tissue, cover your mouth with your arm or shirtsleeve instead of your hands.
- Avoid touching your eyes, nose, or mouth. Viruses can spread this way.
- Avoid sick people.

---

[2] **respiratory:** related to breathing
[3] **stuffy:** blocked, making it difficult to breathe

[4] **immunity:** the ability to not get a disease
[5] **vaccine:** a medicine given to people to protect them from a particular disease

**B.** Circle the answer to each question.

1. What is the purpose of this Web page?
   a. To provide detailed information about flu deaths around the world.
   b. To tell readers how to stay healthy and why they should get a vaccine.
   c. To provide basic information about the flu and how to prevent it.
   d. To scare readers so that they get the flu vaccine every year.

2. Why do people often think a cold is the flu?
   a. Flu symptoms are more severe than cold symptoms.
   b. Cold and flu symptoms can be similar.
   c. A cold only lasts about a week.
   d. Viruses cause colds and the flu.

3. Why is it important to avoid people who are sick with the flu?
   a. They could infect you with the flu.
   b. They should stay in bed.
   c. You may spread a cold to them and make them sicker.
   d. They might not have washed their hands.

4. Based on the information from the FAQs, which of the following can you infer?
   a. Governments give free flu vaccines.
   b. People don't know what the flu is.
   c. The flu is the most difficult global health problem today.
   d. Understanding the flu is important for people around the world.

**C.** Compare a cold and the flu using the Venn diagram below. Write facts about the flu inside the circle on the left. Write facts about a cold inside the circle on the right. Write facts that are true about both a cold and the flu in the middle.

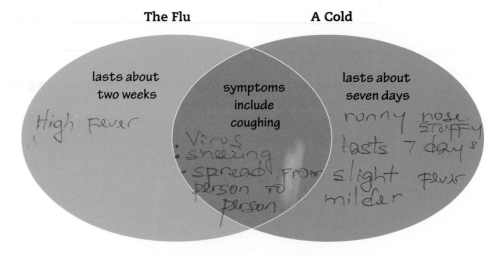

**The Flu**

**A Cold**

lasts about
two weeks

symptoms
include
coughing

lasts about
seven days

High Fever

Virus
sneezing
spread from
person to
person

runny nose
STUFFY
lasts 7 days
slight Fever
milder

**D.** Find the answers to the questions in Reading 1.

1. What percentage of people in the United States gets the flu every year?

   _5 – 20 percent_

2. Why is the flu especially dangerous for elderly people?

   _They may not be able to fight the virus_

3. After you are infected with the flu, how long will it be before you have symptoms?

   _3 – 6 hours_

4. How many deaths are related to the flu worldwide each year?

   _250 000 – 500 000 deaths_

5. What percentage of healthy people under the age of 65 can flu vaccines help in the U.S. every year?

   _70 – 90 percent_

6. How can you prevent the flu from spreading?

   _whash hands , cover nose, Avoid sick people_

**E.** Look back at the reading on pages 174–175 and answer these questions. Then discuss your answers in a group.

1. What is an additional question to add to the FAQ page? Why would this be a good question to add?

   _____

   _____

2. What do you think the answer might be?

   _____

   _____

iQ ONLINE   **F.** Go online to read *The Common Cold* and check your comprehension.

# WRITE WHAT YOU THINK

**A.** Discuss these questions in a group.

1. The reading gives tips on how to avoid getting a cold or the flu. What are some other things you can do?

2. Some people worry a lot about catching the flu from others, and some people are not very concerned. How concerned are you, on a scale from 1 to 10 (10 = extremely concerned, 1 = not concerned at all)? Explain your answers.

3. What other illnesses or diseases are you interested in learning more about? What do you want to know about them?

**B.** Choose one of the questions and write a response. Look back at your Quick Write on page 174 as you think about what you learned.

Question: _____

My Response: _____

_____

_____

---

**Reading Skill** | **Synthesizing information**

When you **synthesize** information, you develop a new understanding about a topic by using information from more than one source. For example, you can synthesize information from two different readings to answer a question. You can also synthesize what you already know about a topic and the new information you are learning about that topic from an article you are reading.

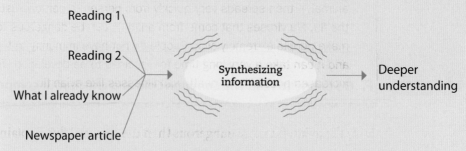

Synthesizing information helps you deepen and expand your knowledge. It is also important because some test questions and writing assignments ask you to synthesize information you have read.

**A. Answer these questions.**

1. Think back to Reading 1. What information in the reading was new to you? What information did you already know?

   _____

   _____

2. Read these questions about Reading 1. Which one is a **synthesis** question? Which is a **main idea** question? Which is a **detail** question? Label each one.

   a. _____ How does the flu spread?

   b. _____ After reading this Web page, will you change any of your health habits? Why or why not?

   c. _____ How many people worldwide have a severe case of the flu every year?

3. Answer the questions in item 2. For the synthesis question, be sure to use information that you already know and information from the reading.

   a. _____

   b. _____

   c. _____

**B. Read this paragraph. Then answer the synthesis questions, using what you already know, information in the paragraph, and the information in Reading 1.**

> Just like humans, animals get flu viruses, too. These animal viruses rarely spread to humans, but occasionally they do. For example, an avian flu, also called bird flu, can spread from birds to humans. Once a person gets a virus from an animal, it then spreads very quickly from person to person, just like other types of the flu. Flu viruses that come from animals can be dangerous to humans and can make people extremely sick. People do not have immunity to these new viruses, and it can take a very long time for vaccines to be developed. There is often an increased possibility of death with illnesses like avian flu.

1. Is the avian flu more dangerous than the seasonal flu? Explain your answer.

   _____

   _____

2. How do you think that avian flu can spread from an animal to a human? How does it spread to many people?

_____

_____

 **iQ** **ONLINE**  **C.** **Go online for more practice with synthesizing information.**

# READING 2 | Watching Over the Health of Millions

 **UNIT OBJECTIVE** ▶▶▶ You are going to read a magazine article about doctors' efforts to prevent the spread of disease at large events. Use the article to gather information and ideas for your Unit Assignment.

## PREVIEW THE READING

**Vocabulary Skill Review**

In Unit 7, you learned about phrasal verbs. Find the two phrasal verbs in paragraph 2 of Reading 1: *show up* and *end up*. Using a dictionary, find out if these phrasal verbs are separable or inseparable.

*strategii*

**A.** **VOCABULARY**  Here are some words from Reading 2. Read their definitions. Then complete each sentence.

> **cooperation** (*noun*) 🔑 working with other people to achieve a goal
>
> **decade** (*noun*) 🔑 a period of ten years
>
> **mass** (*adjective*) 🔑 involving a large number of people
>
> **outbreak** (*noun*) the sudden start of something bad, such as a disease
>
> **quarantine** (*verb*) to keep people who may have a disease away from other people in order to prevent the disease from spreading
>
> **risk** (*noun*) 🔑 the possibility of something bad happening in the future
>
> **strategy** (*noun*) 🔑 a plan that you use to achieve something
>
> **take steps** (*phrasal verb*) to do a series of actions (to achieve something)
>
> **track** (*verb*) 🔑 to find somebody/something by following the signs or information that they have left behind
>
> **vaccination** (*noun*) the injection of a special medicine to protect people from getting a disease

🔑 Oxford 3000™ words

1. All of the students were required to get a _vaccination_ against tuberculosis, a serious disease.

2. Health officials held a _mass_ meeting of thousands of doctors to discuss the problem.

3. Many sick people arrived on the plane. The health officials decided to _quarantine_ all of them in a hospital to keep the disease from spreading.

4. Smoking cigarettes will increase your _____risk_____ of getting lung cancer.

5. The scientists tried to _____track_____ the disease back to its original source.

6. Health is not just a local issue. It is a global issue and requires international _____cooperation_____.

7. It has taken us over a _____decade_____ of hard work to stop the disease from spreading.

8. In the elementary school, there was an _____outbreak_____ of the flu. About 30 percent of the kids got sick.

9. Researchers are trying to develop a good _____strategy_____ to keep people healthy in large groups.

10. The doctors knew that they had to _____take steps_____ immediately to prevent the disease from spreading.

iQ ONLINE **B.** Go online for more practice with the vocabulary.

**C.** PREVIEW You are going to read a magazine article about health problems that occur when there are large groups of people together. At such events, doctors work to prevent diseases from spreading. What do you think that doctors do to try to stop diseases from spreading?

☐ share knowledge      ☑ wash their hands
☐ use technology      ☐ cooperate with others

**D.** QUICK WRITE Diseases can spread quickly in public areas. What do you do to keep health problems from spreading? Think about what you do when you are at school, in a shopping mall, or on an airplane. Write a paragraph about the topic. Be sure to use this section for your Unit Assignment.

# WORK WITH THE READING

**A.** Read the magazine article and gather information about how we can prevent diseases.

# Watching Over the Health of Millions

1    Imagine you are a doctor specializing in infectious disease. Question: What is your worst nightmare[1]? Answer: A huge gathering of people from all over the world, with many sick or elderly people. Why? Because in this very crowded situation, diseases can spread rapidly and uncontrollably.

2    **Mass** gatherings, events with huge crowds of people, happen every year around the world, from the Hajj in Saudi Arabia to the World Cup. Global health experts realize that these mass gatherings can present serious health **risks** and can increase the spread of epidemics. Now doctors from many countries are sharing their knowledge about these health issues and are working together to find solutions.

3    In a recent report, experts from the Saudi Arabian Ministry of Health shared their knowledge about how to prevent the **outbreak** of global diseases at mass gatherings. The Ministry has **decades** of experience in managing the health of pilgrims[2] in the yearly Hajj to Mecca in Saudi Arabia. With more than two million pilgrims each year, the Hajj is the largest international mass gathering in the world. Many of the pilgrims arrive from low-income countries and have had little health care. Elderly or sick pilgrims want to complete this very important religious pilgrimage before they die, so they travel to Mecca with thousands of others.

4    According to the report, one of the first **strategies** is to make sure that all pilgrims receive a health screening[3]. Saudi health experts have designed special programs to screen pilgrims quickly and efficiently. For example, there is a separate terminal at the Jeddah International Airport for pilgrims. When pilgrims arrive by plane, they receive a health screening

and **vaccinations**, if needed. There is a medical clinic at the airport for sick pilgrims. For pilgrims traveling within Saudi Arabia, officials check vaccination records and make sure people are up to date on all required vaccines.

5    Another important Saudi strategy is to use technology to **track** the outbreak of diseases. With many new technologies, experts are able to immediately report a person with a disease. That information quickly goes to all health officials, and organizers can **take steps** to control the outbreak. During a mass gathering, instant reporting is extremely important. During the 2009 Hajj, there was a global outbreak of the H1N1 bird flu pandemic[4]. Hajj organizers used technology to track and report cases of the flu. They used a cell phone system to collect information and the Internet to send reports instantly. Organizers also worked with the World Health Organization (WHO) to use rapid testing and to **quarantine** infected pilgrims. They were able to control the outbreak and prevent the spread to thousands of pilgrims.

6    The field of health for mass gatherings is growing. This is a very new field of medicine, and international **cooperation** is a key ingredient. The Saudi Ministry of Health has recently created a new diploma course in Mass Gathering and Disaster Medicine, based in Jeddah. The goal is to develop an international center for sharing knowledge. Zaid Memish from the Ministry of Health said that "multinational approaches to public health challenges are likely to become major factors in global health diplomacy and bringing the West a little closer to the East." International cooperation will help limit the spread of disease and lead to better health around the world.

---

[1] **nightmare:** a dream that is frightening
[2] **pilgrims:** people who travel to a holy place for religious reasons
[3] **health screening:** the testing or examining of a person for disease
[4] **pandemic:** outbreak of a disease that occurs in many areas of the world at one time

**B. Answer these questions.**

1. Why are large gatherings of people a doctor's nightmare?

   *Because in this very crowded situation diseases can spread rapidly and uncontrollably.*

2. What are some examples of mass gatherings?

   *Huge crowds of people; Hajj; Wold cup*

3. What is the largest international mass gathering in the world?

   *The Hajj is the largest international mas gathering in the world.*

4. What is the first strategy to keep pilgrims healthy?

   *Health screening.*

5. Why is it important to quarantine people who are infected?

   *prevent the spread*

6. What is the second strategy that Saudis use?

   *Created a New Diploma course in Mass gathering an Disaster Medicine (Technology)*

**C. Read the statements. Write *T* (true) or *F* (false). Then correct each false statement to make it true.**

*F* 1. Mass gatherings can present health problems because they decrease the spread of diseases.
   *increase*
   *diseases can spread rapidly and uncontrollably*

*F* 2. The Saudi Arabian Ministry of Health has many years of experience managing people at the Olympic Games.
   *The Hajj, not olympic Games.*

*T* 3. The yearly Hajj brings together about two million people every year.

   _____

*F* 4. The pilgrims are from Saudi Arabia.

   _____

*T* 5. During Hajj, when pilgrims arrive by plane, they must have a health screening.

   _____

<u>F</u> 6. In 2008, there was an outbreak of the H1N1 flu.

2009

<u>F</u> 7. New technology is very helpful in tracking and reporting doctors.

The disease          NOT ↗

<u>T</u> 8. The special field of health for mass gatherings depends on international cooperation.

**D. Complete the paragraphs below with details from the reading.**

Large gatherings of people are dangerous because diseases can spread __rapidly__ and __uncontrollably__ But doctors
               1                    2

from around the world are __sharing__ their knowledge. Many
                            3

pilgrims to the Hajj have had little __health__ care. So health
                                       4

officials first provide a health __screening__ . There is a medical
                                   5

__clinic__ at the airport for pilgrims who are sick. The officials
   6

want to reduce the __risk__ of diseases spreading.
                     7

Saudi officials use __technology__ to track the outbreak of diseases.
                      8

They work with the World Health __organization__ to use rapid testing.
                                  9

Health for mass gatherings is a new __field__ of medicine.
                                      10

**E. What is the author's purpose in this reading? More than one answer is possible.**
   a. to tell an interesting story
   b. to make the reader laugh
   (c.) to give information
   (d.) to explain a situation
   e. to make the reader excited about the topic

# WRITE WHAT YOU THINK

**A. Discuss these questions in a group. Look back at your Quick Write on page 181 as you think about what you learned.**

1. Many people attend mass gatherings even if they are sick. Does this surprise you? Do you think that this should be permitted?

2. What else can doctors and other health care workers do at mass gatherings to help stop the spread of disease?

**B.** Go online to watch the video about avian bird flu. Then check your comprehension.

**CDC** *(n.)* Centers for Disease Control and Prevention, a U.S. government organization

**sustained** *(adj.)* continuous

**vulnerable** *(adj.)* weak and easily hurt physically or emotionally

**Critical Thinking Tip**

Activity C asks you to **recommend** ways to prevent a problem. **Recommending** can help you think through a problem and its possible solutions.

**C.** Think about the unit video, Reading 1, and Reading 2 as you discuss these questions. Then choose one question and write a response.

1. Imagine that an epidemic spreads quickly and becomes a global pandemic. What kinds of problems do you think governments and doctors will face?

2. The flu can spread rapidly in schools and cause teachers and children to become sick. What can a school do to prevent the spread of the flu? When should a school close due to sickness?

## Vocabulary Skill   Collocations

A **collocation** is a group of words that frequently go together. Some collocations are made up of a verb + a preposition. Here are some common collocations with the prepositions *on*, *to*, and *in*.

> comment on: to give an opinion about something
>
> contribute to: to give a part to the total of something
>
> in common: like or similar to somebody or something
>
> increase in: a rise in the number, amount, or level of something
>
> in favor of: in agreement with someone or something
>
> in response to: an answer or reaction to something
>
> participate in: to share or join in
>
> succeed in: to manage to achieve what you want; to do well

Using collocations will help your speaking and writing sound more natural.

**A. Complete each sentence below with the correct collocation.**

| comment on | in common | in favor of | participate in |
|---|---|---|---|
| contribute to | increase in | in response to | succeed in |

1.  A cold and the flu have some things _in common_. For example, they can both be passed from one person to another.

2.  My mother told me she liked my new dress, but she didn't _comment on_ my new haircut. Maybe she doesn't like it.

3.  The scientists need 50 people to _participate in_ a study for a new flu vaccine. They will pay each person $500.

4.  There's been a(n) _increase in_ cases of the flu this winter. It's much worse than last year.

5.  Eating lots of green vegetables can _contribute to_ your overall health.

6.  Sofia nodded her head _in response to_ my question.

7.  If you want to _succeed in_ becoming an Olympic athlete, you have to train very hard.

8.  Keiko was not _in favor of_ the new proposal, so she voted against it.

**B. Choose five collocations from Activity A. Write a sentence using each one. Then share your sentences with a group.**

 **C. Go online for more practice with collocations.**

# WRITING

**UNIT OBJECTIVE** ▶▶▶▶ At the end of this unit, you will create an FAQ (Frequently Asked Questions) page that begins with an explanatory paragraph about an illness. This FAQ page will include specific information from the readings and your own ideas.

## Writing Skill | Writing an explanatory paragraph

An **explanatory paragraph** defines and explains a term or concept. Use an explanatory paragraph when you want to explain a term or concept that your reader might not know.

Use these guidelines to make your explanatory paragraph clear to your reader.

- First, write a topic sentence that states and defines the term or concept.
- Make sure the definition is clear. Use a dictionary or online sources.
- Then write about the term or concept using explanations and examples.
- Explain how the term or concept is different from similar terms.
- Explain what the term or concept is not.

You can use these sentence structures to write a topic sentence for an explanatory paragraph.

_____ is a _____ that _____.

An <u>inhaler</u> is a <u>device</u> that <u>helps a person with asthma breathe</u>.

_____ is when _____.

An <u>epidemic</u> is when <u>many people have an illness at the same time</u>.

**A.** **WRITING MODEL** Read the model explanatory paragraph. Then answer the questions on page 188.

A pandemic is an epidemic that has spread to several countries or continents, becoming a global health emergency. An epidemic can develop into a pandemic very quickly. For example, in 2003, the SARS (Severe Acute Respiratory Syndrome) virus spread from China to 37 countries around the world in just a few weeks. The avian flu caused a pandemic in recent years. In 2009, a new type of flu virus started in Mexico and spread to 70 countries in eight weeks. A month later, the number of countries nearly doubled. A pandemic is not the same as a plague, which is a disease that spreads quickly and kills many people. A pandemic can kill many people, but it doesn't always. However, a pandemic is a very serious international health emergency.

1. What is the definition of *pandemic*?

   _____

2. What term is *pandemic* similar to?

   _____

3. What examples of pandemics does the writer give?

   _____

4. What does the writer say a pandemic is not?

   _____

5. Compare the paragraph on page 187 with paragraph 1 in Reading 1 on page 174. How are the paragraphs similar? How are they different?

   _____

**B.** Write a topic sentence for an explanatory paragraph for each of these topics. Use the two different sentence structures in the skill box on page 187. You may also need to look in the dictionary.

1. A common cold _____

   _____

2. An epidemic _____

   _____

3. Asthma _____

   _____

4. A vaccination _____

   _____

**C.** Complete each of the sentences related to the four topics in Activity B. The sentences will help explain your topic by saying what it is NOT or by using contrast.

1. _A common cold_ is not the same as the flu, _which is_ a more severe illness.

2. Although _____ is similar to the flu, flu

   symptoms are more _____.

3. Like _____, a pandemic is the spread of an infectious disease. However, in _____, the number of people affected is much smaller.

4. _____ is not the same as bronchitis, _____ a very bad cough. Unlike _____, bronchitis is treated with antibiotics.

5. A _____ is a special type of medicine, while *injection* refers to any type of medicine that is given with a needle under the skin. In fact, there are some _____ that are given by mouth, not by injection.

**Writing Tip**

In Activity D, you will complete an idea map to brainstorm ideas. Brainstorming ideas in this way will result in better writing.

**D.** Choose one of the topics in Activity B and complete the idea map to plan your writing. For examples, you can list symptoms or characteristics, depending on your topic.

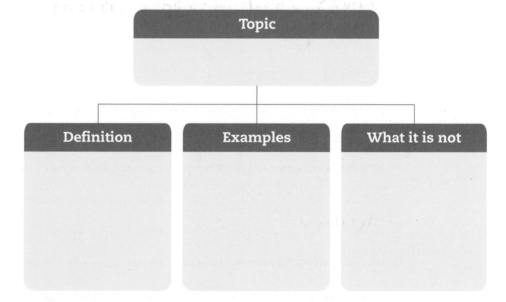

| Topic |
| Definition | Examples | What it is not |

**E.** Write your explanatory paragraph. Use the guidelines in the Writing Skill box, topics from Activity B, and your idea map in Activity D.

**F.** Share your paragraph with another student who wrote about the same topic. Compare your paragraphs. Discuss these questions.

1. How are your topic sentences different? Which topic sentence is stronger? Why?

2. How many examples are in each of your paragraphs? Which examples are similar?

_____

3. Compare each other's sentences that say what your topic is not. How are they different? How do you think this information helps the reader?

_____

**G.** Work together with your partner to write a new explanatory paragraph. Use the best parts of each of your paragraphs.

 **H.** Go online for more practice with explanatory paragraphs.

## Grammar | Adverbs of manner and degree

An **adverb of manner** describes how something is done or how something happens. It usually comes after the verb or object.

> Our team played **hard** and won the game **easily**.
>    verb   adverb   verb   object  adverb

In sentences with an auxiliary verb, *-ly* adverbs of manner can come between the auxiliary verb and the main verb.

> His temperature was **rapidly** rising during the afternoon.
>    auxiliary   adverb   verb

An **adverb of degree** tells to what degree something is done or happens. It comes before an adjective or before another adverb.

> It was an **especially** difficult exam.
>    adverb   adjective

> The man was breathing **fairly** slowly.
>    adverb   adverb

Here are some common adverbs of degree:

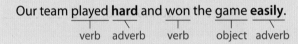

**greater degree**                                  **lesser degree**

extremely  especially  very  really  so  fairly  quite  pretty  somewhat  hardly

**A.** Write the adverb form of each of the adjectives below. Then complete the sentences with the correct adverb of manner.

common__ly__          precise__ly__
efficient__ly__        rapid _____ _rapidly_____
frequent__ly__         serious __ly__
immediate__ly__        successful__ly__

1. The temperature in New York can change very _____ _rapidly_____.
   One day it's warm. The next day it's cold.

2. Doctors have not been able to _Successfuly_ cure the common cold.

3. Modern cars use fuel more _____ than older cars do.

4. Hatem followed the instructions _precisely_, because he didn't want to make a mistake.

5. Maria talks to her family _Frequenly_. She calls them three or four times a week.

6. I need to think about the situation very _seriously_ before I make a decision.

7. The doctor told Anita that her problem was serious. She needed to go to the hospital _immediately_.

8. Orange trees are not _commonly_ found in cold places.

**Tip** for Success

Don't overuse the adverbs *very* and *really*. They are useful general terms, but more specific adverbs give more information and make your writing more interesting.

**B.** Complete the sentences with your own ideas and opinions. Then read your sentences to a partner.

1. I think _____ is really interesting.

2. In my opinion _____ is extremely _____.

3. I can _____ fairly well.

4. For me _____ is extremely difficult.

5. I have had a(n) _____ _____ day today.

**C.** Go online for more practice with adverbs of manner and degree.

**D.** Go online for the grammar expansion.

**Create an FAQ (Frequently Asked Questions) page**

In this assignment, you will write an FAQ (Frequently Asked Questions) page about an illness. You will include an explanation of the topic and information on how the illness can be prevented. As you prepare your FAQ page, think about the Unit Question, "How can we prevent diseases?" Use information from Reading 1, Reading 2, the unit video, and your work in this unit to support your writing. Refer to the Self-Assessment checklist on page 194.

Go to the Online Writing Tutor for a writing model and alternate Unit Assignments.

## PLAN AND WRITE

**A.  Complete these activities.**

1. Brainstorm a list for each question. Write down as many ideas as you can.
   - What illnesses do you know of that can spread from person to person?
   - What are some illnesses that you or someone you know have had?
   - What illnesses have you learned about recently?

2. Discuss your ideas with a partner.

3. Choose the illness you are going to write about.

**Tip for Success**

When you write an FAQ page, keep your audience in mind. Your questions should be questions that the average person might have. Your answers should be informative, but not too long. Be sure to include useful and interesting information that a reader may not know.

**B. PLAN Organize the information about your topic. Remember, your goal is to provide useful information to your readers.**

1. Fill in these FAQs with the illness you chose. Then write notes to answer each question.

   a. What is _____?

   _____

   _____

   b. What are the symptoms of _____?

   _____

   _____

   c. How is _____ different from other diseases?

   _____

   _____

d. Who gets _____?

_____

_____

e. How does _____ spread?

_____

_____

f. How can you avoid getting _____?

_____

_____

g. How can we prevent the spread of _____?

_____

_____

2. Look at your notes. Are there any questions you will not include? Are there any additional questions that you want to include? Make any changes needed.

3. What additional information do you need? Where can you get that information? Find the information you need and add it to your notes.

**C.** **WRITE** Use your **PLAN** notes to write your FAQ page. Go to *iQ Online* to use the Online Writing Tutor.

1. Write your FAQ page, using your notes in Activity B. Start with an explanatory paragraph that clearly explains the illness. Then continue with other questions and answers. Try to use some adverbs of manner and degree.

2. Look at the Self-Assessment checklist on page 194 to guide your writing.

# REVISE AND EDIT

**A.** **PEER REVIEW** Read your partner's FAQ page. Then go online and use the Peer Review worksheet. Discuss the review with your partner.

**B.** **REWRITE** Based on your partner's review, revise and rewrite your paragraph.

**C.** **EDIT** Complete the Self-Assessment checklist as you prepare to write the final draft of your FAQ page. Be prepared to hand in your work or discuss it in class.

| SELF-ASSESSMENT | | |
|:---:|:---:|:---|
| **Yes** | **No** | |
| ☐ | ☐ | Did you clearly define the illness with explanations and examples? |
| ☐ | ☐ | Do you have a good variety of adverbs of manner and degree? Did you use the correct word order? |
| ☐ | ☐ | Did you use collocations to make your writing sound more natural? |
| ☐ | ☐ | Does the FAQ page include vocabulary from the unit? |
| ☐ | ☐ | Did you check the FAQ page for punctuation, spelling, and grammar? |

**D.** **REFLECT** Go to the Online Discussion Board to discuss these questions.

1. What is something new you learned in this unit?

2. Look back at the Unit Question—How can we prevent diseases? Is your answer different now than when you started the unit? If yes, how is it different? Why?

# TRACK YOUR SUCCESS

**Circle the words and phrases you have learned in this unit.**

**Nouns**
cooperation 🔑 AWL
decade 🔑 AWL
epidemic
outbreak
risk 🔑
strategy 🔑 AWL
symptom
vaccination
virus 🔑

**Verbs**
cover 🔑
develop 🔑

infect 🔑
quarantine
track 🔑

**Adjectives**
mass 🔑
severe 🔑

**Adverbs**
approximately 🔑 AWL
extremely 🔑

**Phrasal Verbs**
take steps

**Collocations**
comment on
contribute to
in common
increase in
in favor of
in response to
participate in
related to 🔑
succeed in

🔑 Oxford 3000™ words
AWL Academic Word List

**Check (✓) the skills you learned. If you need more work on a skill, refer to the page(s) in parentheses.**

| | |
|---|---|
| **READING** ☐ | I can synthesize information. (p. 178) |
| **VOCABULARY** ☐ | I can use collocations. (p. 185) |
| **WRITING** ☐ | I can write an explanatory paragraph. (p. 187) |
| **GRAMMAR** ☐ | I can use adverbs of manner and degree. (p. 190) |
| **UNIT OBJECTIVE** ▶▶▶▶ ☐ | I can gather information and ideas to create an FAQ page that begins with an explanatory paragraph about an illness. |

# AUTHORS AND CONSULTANTS

## Authors

**Joe McVeigh** holds a B.A. in English and American Literature from Brown University and an M.A. in TESOL from Biola University. He has taught at Middlebury College, the University of Southern California, the California Institute of Technology, and California State University, Los Angeles. Joe has also lived and worked overseas in the U.K., Hungary, China, India, Chile, and the Middle East. He has presented nationally and internationally on topics including methods and techniques for teaching English, intercultural communication, and curriculum development. He works independently as a consultant, teacher-trainer, workshop presenter, and author.

**Jennifer Bixby** holds an M.A. in TESOL from Boston University. She is a senior development editor for EF Englishtown, editing and writing online ELT content. Jennifer has taught students of various ages in Colombia, Japan, and the U.S in a wide variety of programs, including community colleges and intensive English programs. She has presented at numerous conferences on the topics of materials development and the teaching of reading and writing. She is coauthor with Nigel Caplan of *Inside Writing* 2 and 4 published by Oxford University Press.

## Series Consultants

### ONLINE INTEGRATION

**Chantal Hemmi** holds an Ed.D. TEFL and is a Japan-based teacher trainer and curriculum designer. Since leaving her position as Academic Director of the British Council in Tokyo, she has been teaching at the Center for Language Education and Research at Sophia University on an EAP/CLIL program offered for undergraduates. She delivers lectures and teacher trainings throughout Japan, Indonesia, and Malaysia.

### COMMUNICATIVE GRAMMAR

**Nancy Schoenfeld** holds an M.A. in TESOL from Biola University in La Mirada, California, and has been an English language instructor since 2000. She has taught ESL in California and Hawaii, and EFL in Thailand and Kuwait. She has also trained teachers in the United States and Indonesia. Her interests include teaching vocabulary, extensive reading, and student motivation. She is currently an English Language Instructor at Kuwait University.

### WRITING

**Marguerite Ann Snow** holds a Ph.D. in Applied Linguistics from UCLA. She teaches in the TESOL M.A. program in the Charter College of Education at California State University, Los Angeles. She was a Fulbright scholar in Hong Kong and Cyprus. In 2006, she received the President's Distinguished Professor award at Cal State, LA. She has trained EFL teachers in Algeria, Argentina, Brazil, Egypt, Libya, Morocco, Pakistan, Peru, Spain, and Turkey. She is the author/editor of publications in the areas of integrated content, English for academic purposes, and standards for English teaching and learning. She recently served as a co-editor of *Teaching English as a Second or Foreign Language* (4th ed.).

### VOCABULARY

**Cheryl Boyd Zimmerman** is a Professor at California State University, Fullerton. She specializes in second-language vocabulary acquisition, an area in which she is widely published. She teaches graduate courses on second-language acquisition, culture, vocabulary, and the fundamentals of TESOL and is a frequent invited speaker on topics related to vocabulary teaching and learning. She is the author of *Word Knowledge: A Vocabulary Teacher's Handbook* and Series Director of *Inside Reading, Inside Writing,* and *Inside Listening and Speaking,* all published by Oxford University Press.

### ASSESSMENT

**Lawrence J. Zwier** holds an M.A. in TESL from the University of Minnesota. He is currently the Associate Director for Curriculum Development at the English Language Center at Michigan State University in East Lansing. He has taught ESL/EFL in the United States, Saudi Arabia, Malaysia, Japan, and Singapore.

iQ ONLINE extends your learning beyond the classroom. This online content is specifically designed for you! *iQ Online* gives you flexible access to essential content.

Activities include
• Additional **practice** and support
• **Videos**—watch anytime, anywhere
• **Online tests** assigned by your teacher.

Progress reports show what skills you have learned and where you still need more practice.

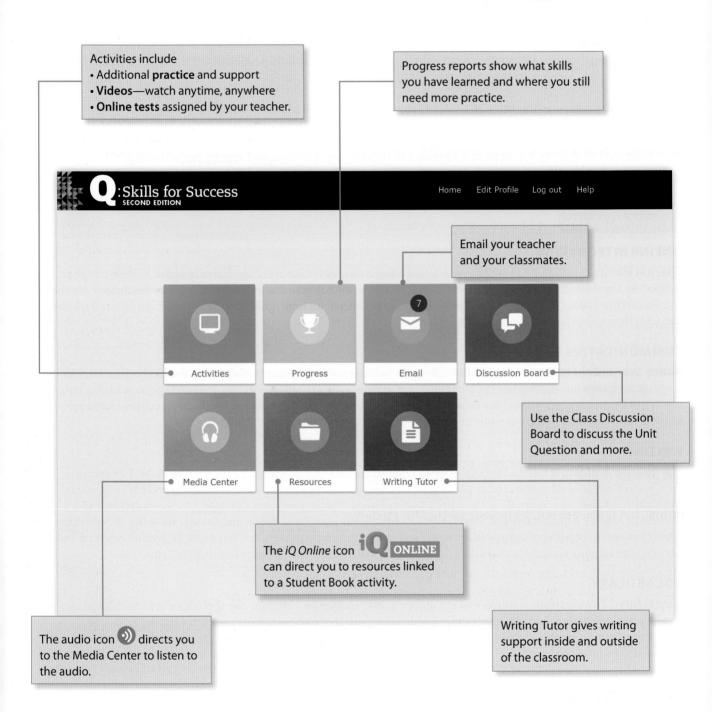

Email your teacher and your classmates.

Use the Class Discussion Board to discuss the Unit Question and more.

The *iQ Online* icon can direct you to resources linked to a Student Book activity.

The audio icon directs you to the Media Center to listen to the audio.

Writing Tutor gives writing support inside and outside of the classroom.

**SEE THE INSIDE FRONT COVER FOR HOW TO REGISTER FOR *iQ ONLINE* FOR THE FIRST TIME.**

## Take Control of Your Learning

You have the choice of where and how you complete the activities. Access your activities and view your progress at any time.

Your teacher may

- assign *iQ Online* as homework,
- do the activities with you in class, or
- let you complete the activities at a pace that is right for you.

*iQ Online* makes it easy to access everything you need.

## Set Clear Goals

**STEP 1** If it is your first time, look through the site. See what learning opportunities are available.

**STEP 2** The Student Book provides the framework and purpose for each online activity. Before going online, notice the goal of the exercises you are going to do.

**STEP 3** Stay on top of your work, following the teacher's instructions.

**STEP 4** Use *iQ Online* for review. You can use the materials any time. It is easy for you to do follow-up activities when you have missed a class or want to review.

## Manage Your Progress

The activities in *iQ Online* are designed for you to work independently. You can become a confident learner by monitoring your progress and reviewing the activities at your own pace. You may already be used to working online, but if you are not, go to your teacher for guidance.

Check 'View Reports' to monitor your progress. The reports let you track your own progress at a glance. Think about your own performance and set new goals that are right for you, following the teacher's instructions.

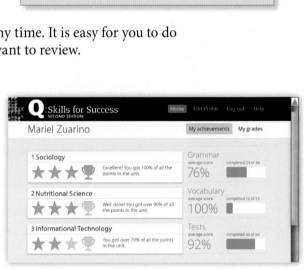

Notice the icon. It directs you to the online materials linked to the Student Book activities.

*iQ Online* is a research-based solution specifically designed for English language learners that extends learning beyond the classroom. I hope these steps help you make the most of this essential content.

Chantal Hemmi, EdD TEFL
Center for Language Education and Research
Sophia University, Japan

# AUDIO TRACK LIST

))) *Q: Skills for Success Second Edition* audio can be found in the Media Center.

Follow these steps:

**Step 1:** Go to iQOnlinePractice.com.

**Step 2:** Click on the Media Center icon. 🎧

**Step 3:** Choose to stream or download ⬇ the audio file you select. Not all audio files are available for download.

**Class Audio**

| Unit | Page | Listen | Download |
|------|------|--------|----------|
| **Unit 1** | | | |
| 1 | 3 | The Q Classroom | ⬇ |
| 1 | 6 | Work With the Reading | ⬇ |
| 1 | 13 | Work With the Reading | ⬇ |
| **Unit 2** | | | |
| 2 | 28 | The Q Classroom | ⬇ |
| 2 | 32 | Work With the Reading | ⬇ |
| 2 | 38 | Work With the Reading | ⬇ |
| **Unit 3** | | | |
| 3 | 55 | The Q Classroom | ⬇ |
| 3 | 58 | Work With the Reading | ⬇ |
| 3 | 65 | Work With the Reading | |

Back

| Unit | Activity | Track File Name |
|------|----------|-----------------|
| **Unit 1** | The Q Classroom, p. 3 | Q2e_02_RW_U01_Q_Classroom.mp3 |
| | Work With the Reading, p. 6 | Q2e_02_RW_U01_ Reading1.mp3 |
| | Work With the Reading, p. 12 | Q2e_02_RW_U01_Reading2.mp3 |
| **Unit 2** | The Q Classroom, p. 26 | Q2e_02_RW_U02_Q_Classroom.mp3 |
| | Work With the Reading, p. 31 | Q2e_02_RW_U02_Reading1.mp3 |
| | Work With the Reading, p. 37 | Q2e_02_RW_U02_Reading2.mp3 |
| **Unit 3** | The Q Classroom, p. 50 | Q2e_02_RW_U03_Q_Classroom.mp3 |
| | Work With the Reading, p. 54 | Q2e_02_RW_U03_Reading1.mp3 |
| | Work With the Reading, p. 61 | Q2e_02_RW_U03_Reading2.mp3 |
| **Unit 4** | The Q Classroom, p. 74 | Q2e_02_RW_U04_Q_Classroom.mp3 |
| | Work With the Reading, p. 78 | Q2e_02_RW_U04_Reading1.mp3 |
| | Work With the Reading, p. 85 | Q2e_02_RW_U04_Reading2.mp3 |
| **Unit 5** | The Q Classroom, p. 99 | Q2e_02_RW_U05_Q_Classroom.mp3 |
| | Work With the Reading, p. 103 | Q2e_02_RW_U05_Reading1.mp3 |
| | Work With the Reading, p. 109 | Q2e_02_RW_U05_Reading2.mp3 |
| **Unit 6** | The Q Classroom, p. 123 | Q2e_02_RW_U06_Q_Classroom.mp3 |
| | Work With the Reading, p. 126 | Q2e_02_RW_U06_Reading1.mp3 |
| | Work With the Reading, p. 133 | Q2e_02_RW_U06_Reading2.mp3 |
| **Unit 7** | The Q Classroom, p. 146 | Q2e_02_RW_U07_Q_Classroom.mp3 |
| | Work With the Reading, p. 151 | Q2e_02_RW_U07_Reading1.mp3 |
| | Work With the Reading, p. 158 | Q2e_02_RW_U07_Reading2.mp3 |
| **Unit 8** | The Q Classroom, p. 171 | Q2e_02_RW_U08_Q_Classroom.mp3 |
| | Work With the Reading, p. 174 | Q2e_02_RW_U08_Reading1.mp3 |
| | Work With the Reading, p. 182 | Q2e_02_RW_U08_Reading2.mp3 |

The keywords of the **Oxford 3000™** have been carefully selected by a group of language experts and experienced teachers as the words which should receive priority in vocabulary study because of their importance and usefulness.

**AWL** **The Academic Word List** is the most principled and widely accepted list of academic words. Averil Coxhead gathered information from academic materials across the academic disciplines to create this word list.

**The Common European Framework of Reference for Languages (CEFR)** provides a basic description of what language learners have to do to use language effectively. The system contains 6 reference levels: **A1, A2, B1, B2, C1, C2**. CEFR leveling provided by the Word Family Framework, created by Richard West and published by the British Council. http://www.learnenglish.org.uk/wff/

## UNIT 1

clear *(adj.)*, A1
connect *(v.)*, A2
contribute *(v.)* AWL, A2
express *(v.)*, A1
find out *(phr. v.)*, A2
influence *(v.)*, A2
psychologist *(n.)* AWL, B1
purchase *(n.)* AWL, B1
recommend *(v.)*, A2
researcher *(n.)* AWL, A2
review *(n.)*, A2
social *(adj.)*, A1
spread *(v.)*, A2
study *(n.)*, A1
trend *(n.)* AWL, A2

## UNIT 2

advertising *(n.)*, B1
affect *(v.)* AWL, A1
consider *(v.)*, A1
culture *(n.)* AWL, A1
dependable *(adj.)*, B1
emotion *(n.)*, A2
encourage *(v.)*, A1
environment *(n.)* AWL, A1
establish *(v.)* AWL, A1
psychological *(adj.)* AWL, B1

represent *(v.)*, B1
service *(n.)*, A2
specific *(adj.)* AWL, A1
unaware *(adj.)* AWL, B2
universal *(adj.)*, B1
variety *(n.)*, A1

## UNIT 3

advice *(n.)*, A2
avoid *(v.)*, A1
awkward *(adj.)*, B2
manners *(n.)*, B2
appropriately *(adv.)* AWL, B2
behavior *(n.)*, A1
custom *(n.)*, A2
firmly *(adv.)*, B1
informal *(adj.)*, B1
interrupt *(v.)*, B1
make a good impression
    *(phr. v.)*, B2
gesture *(n.)*, B1
respect *(n.)*, A2
take part in *(phr. v.)*, B1
traditional *(adj.)* AWL, A1
typical *(adj.)*, A2

## UNIT 4

advantage *(n.)*, A1
artificial *(adj.)*, B2

ban *(v.)*, B1
championship *(n.)*, A2
compete *(v.)*, A2
effect *(n.)*, A1
energy *(n.)* AWL, A2
equipment *(n.)* AWL, A1
financial *(adj.)* AWL, A1
include *(v.)*, A1
invent *(v.)*, B1
limit *(n.)*, A2
performance *(n.)*, B1
reason *(n.)*, A1
solution *(n.)*, A2
technology *(n.)* AWL, A1

## UNIT 5

challenge *(n.)* AWL, A2
corporation *(n.)* AWL, B1
courage *(n.)*, B2
depend on *(phr. v.)*, A2
design *(v.)* AWL, A1
enthusiasm *(n.)*, B1
expand *(v.)* AWL, A2
expert *(n.)* AWL, A2
goal *(n.)* AWL, A2
lifestyle *(n.)*, B2
manage *(v.)*, A1
pass down *(phr. v.)*, B1

realistic *(adj.)* 🔑, **B1**
responsibility *(n.)* 🔑, **A1**
strength *(n.)* 🔑, **A1**
talent *(n.)* 🔑, **B1**
unity *(n.)*, **B1**

## UNIT 6

automatically *(adv.)* 🔑 AWL, **B1**
access *(n.)* 🔑 AWL, **A1**
assist *(v.)* 🔑 AWL, **B1**
benefit *(n.)* 🔑 AWL, **A1**
blame *(v.)* 🔑, **A2**
connection *(n.)* 🔑, **B1**
decrease *(v.)* 🔑, **B1**
error *(n.)* 🔑 AWL, **A2**
estimate *(v.)* 🔑 AWL, **A2**
eventually *(adv.)* 🔑 AWL, **A1**
frustrated *(adj.)*, **B2**
furious *(adj.)*, **B2**
install *(v.)* 🔑, **B1**
interact *(v.)* AWL, **B2**
on hold *(phr.)*, **B2**
provide *(v.)* 🔑, **A1**
scan *(v.)*, **B2**

stressed *(adj.)* 🔑 AWL, **B1**
transfer *(v.)* 🔑 AWL, **B1**
unique *(adj.)* 🔑 AWL, **A2**

## UNIT 7

actual *(adj.)* 🔑, **A2**
attitude *(n.)* 🔑 AWL, **A1**
budget *(n.)* 🔑, **A1**
consequences *(n.)* 🔑 AWL, **A2**
consumer *(n.)* 🔑 AWL, **A1**
disposable *(adj.)* AWL, **B1**
exist *(v.)* 🔑, **A1**
factor *(n.)* 🔑 AWL, **A1**
feature *(n.)* 🔑 AWL, **A1**
fresh *(adj.)* 🔑, **A2**
habit *(n.)* 🔑, **B1**
materialistic *(adj.)*, **B2**
model *(n.)* 🔑, **A2**
patched *(adj.)*, **B2**
persuade *(v.)* 🔑, **A2**
possession *(n.)* 🔑, **B2**
sign *(n.)* 🔑, **A2**
significant *(adj.)* 🔑 AWL, **A1**
term *(n.)* 🔑, **A2**

## UNIT 8

approximately *(adv.)* 🔑 AWL, **B1**
cooperation *(n.)* 🔑 AWL, **B1**
cover *(v.)* 🔑, **A2**
decade *(n.)* 🔑 AWL, **A2**
develop *(v.)* 🔑, **A1**
epidemic *(n.)*, **C1**
extremely *(adv.)* 🔑, **A2**
infect *(v.)* 🔑, **B1**
mass *(adj.)* 🔑, **B1**
outbreak *(n.)*, **C1**
quarantine *(v.)*, **C1**
related to *(adj.)* 🔑, **B1**
risk *(n.)* 🔑, **A1**
strategy *(n.)* 🔑 AWL, **A1**
severe *(adj.)* 🔑, **A2**
symptom *(n.)*, **B1**
take steps *(phr. v.)*, **A2**
track *(v.)* 🔑, **B1**
vaccination *(n.)*, **C1**
virus *(n.)* 🔑, **B1**